BILAL IQBAL

Childhood Wounds and The Adult Mind

A Scientifically Grounded, Philosophically Honest Exploration of How Early Wounds Shape the Self — and How the Self Can Reshape Itself

First edition

This book was professionally typeset on Reedsy.
Find out more at reedsy.com

For Rahat Iqbal,
my sister, who saw me when I could not see myself,
and who believed I would make it through when I did not.

And for Ali Raza Yaseen,
my best friend, who stayed when staying was difficult,
and whose presence reminded me what friendship actually means.

You both taught me that chosen family is real,
and that love does not always come from where we expect it.

"Out of suffering have emerged the strongest souls; the most massive characters are seared with scars."

- Kahlil Gibran

Contents

Preface

This is a book I wish I had been able to read ten years ago, when I was in the thick of it and did not have the language to understand what was happening inside me. When I thought I was uniquely broken. When I believed that the depression, the hypervigilance, the chronic exhaustion, the difficulty with relationships, the sense of being fundamentally different from everyone around me - when I believed all of that was my fault. Evidence of some essential inadequacy that I needed to hide.

I did not know then what I know now: that I was carrying childhood trauma. That the household I grew up in - marked by domestic violence, emotional neglect, and the kinds of daily unpredictabilities that teach a nervous system to never fully relax - had shaped me in ways that were both invisible and profound. I did not know that the brain adapts to its environment, especially the developing brain of a child, and that my brain had adapted exactly as it should have. That the hypervigilance was not paranoia. The difficulty trusting was not a character flaw. The depression was not laziness. They were the entirely predictable consequences of growing up in a place where safety was scarce.

No one told me this. And so I spent years - a decade, really - believing that I was the problem. That if I just tried harder, thought more positively, was less sensitive, more resilient, less difficult, I would be fine. That everyone else seemed to manage life with relative ease, and my struggle was proof that I was doing something wrong.

It was not until I encountered the research on Adverse Childhood Experiences - the ACE Study - that something shifted. Not immediately. Not all at once. But slowly, over months and years of reading neuroscience and psychology and philosophy, of trying to understand what trauma actually is and what it does to a person, I began to see my own experience with clarity. The patterns made sense. The symptoms were not random. The struggle was not moral failure. It was biology. It was adaptation. It was the entirely reasonable response of a human organism to conditions that were genuinely difficult.

That recognition changed everything. Not because it made the struggle go away - it did not - but because it removed the shame. It gave me a framework. It told me I was not uniquely damaged. That millions of people carry versions of what I carry. That the science was clear, the mechanisms were understood, and more importantly, that change was possible. The brain that had been shaped by trauma could be reshaped by recovery. Slowly. Imperfectly. But genuinely.

This book is written for the person I was then. For anyone who is carrying the weight of a difficult childhood and does not quite know why everything feels so hard. For anyone who has been told they are too sensitive, too anxious, too much, when what they actually are is traumatized. For anyone who is tired of pretending to be fine. For anyone who wants to understand.

I have tried to write the book I needed. One that takes the science seriously without making it inaccessible. One that honors the philosophy - because questions about consciousness, suffering, and the nature of the self are not luxuries, they are central to understanding what it means to be a person carrying trauma. One that does not shy away from the difficulty, but also does not end in despair. One that says clearly: this is what trauma does, this is why it makes sense, and this is what is possible now.

I am not a clinician. I am not a therapist. I am a person who studied biology and philosophy, who worked as a teacher for eight years, who lived through a childhood that shaped me in ways I am still discovering, and who spent a decade in major depression trying to understand why. This book is the synthesis of that understanding. It is grounded in research - hundreds of studies, dozens of theoretical frameworks, the best available science on trauma and the brain. But it is also personal. Because I cannot write about trauma from a purely academic distance. I have lived inside it. And that lived experience is part of what this book offers.

If you are reading this, you probably know something about that lived experience yourself. You know what it feels like to walk into a room and immediately scan for threat. To have relationships that are harder than they should be. To carry a heaviness that other people do not seem to carry. To wonder, sometimes, whether you will ever feel okay.

I want to tell you, plainly and honestly: you are not broken. You are not uniquely damaged. You are not weak for struggling.

What you are is a person whose nervous system was shaped by conditions that required vigilance, self-protection, and enormous effort just to survive. And that nervous system is doing exactly what it was trained to do. The problem is not you. The problem is that the training was for a world that no longer exists - or that exists much less than it used to - and your system has not yet learned to stand down.

It can learn. The research on neuroplasticity, on earned secure attachment, on post-traumatic growth - all of it says that change is real. Not easy. Not quick. But real. The brain that was shaped by adversity can be reshaped by recovery. The patterns that were learned can be unlearned, or at least layered over with new patterns that work better. The life you have now is not the only life available to you.

This book is organized in three parts. Part I examines the wound: how childhood trauma shapes the developing brain, what attachment theory tells us about early relationships, how the self fragments under conditions of sustained threat. Part II explores the weight: the depression that follows trauma, the body that carries what the mind could not hold, the social masks and economic hardships that compound everything else. Part III turns toward possibility: resilience, growth, the capacity to love despite never having been taught how, the philosophical questions about consciousness and suffering, and finally, integration - the life you build in the ruins.

You do not have to read it in order. If you need hope first, start with Part III. If you need validation that what you experienced was real and had real effects, start with Part I. If you need to understand why your body hurts or why relationships are so difficult, those chapters are waiting. This book is a tool. Use it however it serves you.

What I hope you find here is not a cure - there is no cure for having lived through difficult things - but understanding. Context. The recognition that you are not alone in this. And the evidence-backed, science-supported, philosophically-grounded claim that the future does not have to look like the past. That you can learn what you were never taught. That you can heal what was hurt. That the person you are becoming is not doomed by the person you had to be to survive.

You made it this far. Through the childhood that tried to break you, through the years of not understanding why everything was so hard, through the depression and the anxiety and the exhaustion. You picked up a book about trauma and are reading the preface, which means some part of you still believes that understanding is possible. That change is possible. That this, right now, does not have to be permanent.

That part of you - the part that is still asking questions, still seeking, still hoping - is right. Hold onto it. It is going to carry you through what comes next.

- Bilal Iqbal
February 2026

Acknowledgments

This book would not exist without the people who held space for me while I wrote it, who believed in the project when I doubted it, and who reminded me - when I needed reminding - that my story was worth telling.

To my sister, Rahat Iqbal: You have been my witness. You know the house we grew up in, the things we do not speak about, and the weight of carrying what we carry. You have never asked me to be anything other than what I am. That gift - the permission to simply exist without performance - is something I will never be able to adequately thank you for. This book is yours as much as it is mine.

To Ali Raza Yaseen: Friendship, for me, was always a complicated thing. You made it simple. You showed up. You stayed. You did not try to fix me or tell me to be different. You just... were there. Consistently. Reliably. In ways I had not experienced before. You taught me what secure attachment feels like, even if neither of us called it that at the time. Thank you for being the kind of friend I did not know was possible.

To my students over the eight years I taught biology: You do not know this, but many of you saved me. On days when getting out of bed felt impossible, the knowledge that you would be in that classroom waiting - that someone would notice if I did not show up - was often the only reason I went. You thought I was teaching you. But you were teaching me what it meant to be needed, to matter, to have a purpose beyond survival. Some of you still reach out. You still remember me. That matters more than you know.

To the researchers, clinicians, and scholars whose work informed this book: Your rigor gave me a framework when I had none. Your willingness to study difficult things - trauma, attachment, suffering, the long shadow that childhood casts - made it possible for people like me to understand ourselves. This book stands on the foundation you built. Thank you for doing work that matters.

To everyone who has carried the weight of childhood trauma and found the strength to continue: This book is for you. Written by someone who understands, from the inside, what it costs to survive. What it costs to keep going when everything in you wants to stop. What it costs to build a life from ruins. You are not alone in this. And your survival - just your survival, just the fact that you are still here - is already extraordinary.

And finally, to the person I was ten years ago, sitting in the dark, believing that the darkness was permanent: You were wrong about that. It got better. Not easily. Not quickly. But genuinely. I wish I could have told you that then. I hope this book reaches someone who needs to hear it now.

- Bilal Iqbal

I

The Wound

How childhood adversity shapes the brain, body, attachment, and sense of self. Scientific foundation with philosophical depth.

1

The House That Shaped You

How Childhood Environments Become the Architecture of the Mind

"The child is the father of the man - and sometimes, the wound is the foundation."
- William Wordsworth (adapted)

Picture a house. Not a grand one - just an ordinary house, the kind you might walk past a hundred times without looking twice. Peeling paint, maybe. A front door that sticks in winter. A garden that was once somebody's project and is now just weeds. From the outside, you cannot tell much about what happened inside. You cannot tell from the architecture whether the people who lived there were happy or miserable, whether there was laughter at dinner or silence, whether children went to bed feeling safe or spent their nights learning to read the sound of footsteps on the stairs.

Now picture that same house - but understand it as a mind. Because that is what this chapter is going to argue, and what the neuroscience of the last four decades has been quietly, insistently proving: the environment a child grows up in does not merely influence who they become. It builds them. Brick by brick, year by year, the emotional climate of a childhood home becomes the literal architecture of a developing brain. The walls are made of memory. The doors are made of learned behavior. The windows are what we were allowed to see - and the rooms we were locked out of are the things we were never allowed to feel.

This is not a metaphor I am asking you to take on faith. It is biology. And before we go anywhere else in this book - before we talk about depression, or identity, or the long and complicated work of becoming someone who is not just surviving - we need to begin here. At the house. At the beginning.

1.1 - The Developing Brain as a Mirror

There is a question that sounds simple until you really sit with it: what is a brain for? Not in the grand philosophical sense - not yet - but in the plain evolutionary sense. What is this three-pound organ in your skull actually designed to do?

The answer, it turns out, is simpler and stranger than most people expect. The brain is a prediction machine. Its primary job - the thing it is doing all day, every day, mostly without your conscious awareness - is to build models of the world and use those models to predict what is going to happen next. It does this so that you can act before the tiger reaches you rather than after. It does this so that you can navigate a social situation, recognize a friend's face, know that fire is hot without having to put your hand in it every single time.

Karl Friston, one of the most influential neuroscientists alive, describes this as the brain's 'predictive processing' framework. The brain, in his model, is constantly generating predictions about incoming sensory data and then updating those predictions based on what actually arrives. Every moment of your conscious experience is your brain's best guess about what is real - a model of the world, built from experience, continuously revised. The philosopher Andy Clark calls this being a 'prediction machine.' The brain is not a passive receiver of information. It is an active hypothesis-generator, a pattern-detector, a story-maker trying to stay one step ahead of reality.

Now here is where childhood becomes everything.

> *The younger the brain, the more it is being built - not just used. A child's brain is not a small adult brain. It is a fundamentally different kind of organ: one that is, above all else, learning what the world is.*

At birth, the human brain is profoundly unfinished. Unlike most other animals - whose brains come more pre-programmed for their environment - humans are born with the longest window of neural development of any species on earth. This is, from an evolutionary standpoint, a tremendous advantage. It means we are not locked into any particular environment. We can adapt to almost anything. But it also means something that carries enormous weight for this book: the brain that is most adaptable is also the brain that is most vulnerable. The plasticity that allows a child to learn language, recognize faces, and understand social norms is the same plasticity that allows chronic fear, chaos, and neglect to reshape the brain's very structure.

Neuroscientist Bruce Perry, whose work with traumatized children has fundamentally changed how we understand childhood adversity, describes it this way: the brain develops in a 'use-dependent' fashion. The neural pathways that get used most frequently in childhood are the ones that get strengthened, myelinated, made efficient. The ones that go unused wither. This is Hebb's Law at its most basic: neurons that fire together, wire together. And neurons that never fire together disconnect.

What this means, practically, is profound. A child who grows up in a home where emotional attunement is frequent - where a parent regularly recognizes, mirrors, and responds to the child's inner states - develops robust neural pathways for emotional regulation. They build, from thousands of tiny interactions, the brain architecture of someone who can feel a strong emotion without being overwhelmed by it. Who can tolerate uncertainty. Who can trust that the discomfort of the moment will pass.

A child who grows up without that attunement - or worse, in an environment where emotional expression is dangerous - builds different pathways. Not deficient ones, necessarily.

Different ones. Adaptations to a different world. A world where hyper-vigilance is more useful than curiosity. Where closing down is safer than opening up. Where the most important skill is not self-expression but self-protection.

The Most Formative Years Are the Ones You Cannot Remember

Here is a fact that strikes most people as deeply unfair when they first encounter it: the period of development that has the most lasting impact on adult psychology - roughly the first three to five years of life - is almost entirely inaccessible to conscious memory. We call this infantile amnesia, and it is not quite what it sounds like. It is not that nothing is being recorded during those years. Quite the opposite. The brain is recording everything, frantically, voraciously, building its core models of how the world works, how other people behave, what relationships feel like, whether the world is basically safe or basically threatening.

But the memories being formed in early childhood are largely implicit - procedural, emotional, bodily - rather than explicit. They do not get stored as stories you can tell. They get stored as ways your body responds, as assumptions so fundamental they do not feel like assumptions at all. They feel like reality. They feel like the way things are.

This is why the adult who grew up in a chaotic, fearful home does not, as a rule, simply remember their childhood and feel sad about it. They carry that childhood in their nervous system. In their startle response. In the way they tense when someone raises their voice, even in a room full of friends, even when the voice is not angry. In the way they scan a room before they relax into it. These are not dramatic symptoms. They are just the operating system, running in the background, built from a world that no longer exists but that the body still believes in.

✦✦✦

I want to stop here for a moment and say something that might be obvious but feels important to say explicitly. None of this - none of the neuroscience we are about to walk through - is an argument that people are simply products of their childhoods. That you are helpless. That the blueprint is fixed. One of the most important things we will return to, again and again throughout this book, is neuroplasticity: the brain's lifelong capacity to change. The fact that childhood is profoundly shaping does not mean it is permanently determining. These are different claims, and the difference matters enormously.

But we cannot talk honestly about change without first talking honestly about formation. You cannot decide whether to repaint the walls until you can see what was painted in the dark. And seeing clearly - without denial, without drama, with simple scientific honesty - is where this work begins.

1.2 - Domestic Violence and the Nervous System

Let me tell you something about fear. Not the fear you feel when you watch a thriller and the music swells. Not even the fear of a car accident or a sudden shock. I mean the particular kind of fear that lives in a house. The fear that has nowhere to go, because the source of the danger is also the person who is supposed to keep you safe.

That kind of fear is biologically distinct. And what it does to a developing nervous system is something science has been measuring with increasing precision for the last thirty years.

When a child witnesses or experiences violence in the home, the body responds the way bodies always respond to threat: it activates. The amygdala - an almond-shaped cluster of neurons deep in the temporal lobe, the brain's primary threat-detection system - fires. The hypothalamus receives the signal and activates the sympathetic nervous system. The adrenal glands pump cortisol and adrenaline into the bloodstream. Heart rate rises. Breathing shallows. Blood flow redirects from the digestive system and prefrontal cortex toward the major muscle groups. The body prepares to run, or to fight, or - if neither is possible - to freeze.

All of this happens in milliseconds. And all of it, in the context of an acute threat, is exactly the right biological response. The stress-response system exists for a reason. It has kept our species alive. The problem is not the system. The problem is what happens when the system never gets to turn off.

The HPA Axis: Your Body's Alarm That Never Resets

The hypothalamic-pituitary-adrenal axis - the HPA axis - is the brain and body's central stress-regulation system. Think of it as the alarm system of a building. When there is a real threat, the alarm sounds. When the threat passes, the alarm is reset. Calm returns. The system waits.

In a child who grows up in a home where violence is routine, or where the threat of violence is routine - which is almost as damaging, because the nervous system cannot reliably distinguish between threat and the anticipation of threat - the HPA axis is activated repeatedly, sometimes continuously. And here is what happens to an alarm system that goes off too often, for too long, in a developing body: it gets recalibrated. Its baseline shifts. What used to be the 'alarm state' becomes the resting state. The system does not return to calm because, in the world it learned in, calm was not a reasonable prediction. Danger was.

> *Chronic stress does not just make a child anxious. It rewires the system that decides what 'normal' feels like. And once normal is recalibrated toward threat, everything that comes after - relationships, school, adult life - gets filtered through that lens.*

Researcher Martin Teicher at Harvard has spent decades imaging the brains of people who experienced childhood maltreatment. His findings are sobering and important: early adversity does not merely affect how people feel or behave. It produces measurable, lasting differences in brain structure - in the corpus callosum (which connects the two hemispheres), in the prefrontal cortex (responsible for reasoning, planning, and impulse control), and in the neural pathways that connect the limbic system to the cortex. These are not signs of damage in the way a broken bone is damage. They are signs of adaptation - a brain that reorganized itself around a particular kind of world. But adaptations to a dangerous childhood can look like pathology in a safer adult life.

What It Means When Fear Becomes the Operating System

There is a phrase I want to introduce here that we will return to many times in this book: the window of tolerance. Psychologist Dan Siegel describes it as the zone of arousal within which a person can function effectively - engaged enough to be present, calm enough to think clearly. Within this window, we can process difficult emotions without being overwhelmed by them. We can be curious about our experience rather than just reactive to it.

Children raised in violent or unpredictable homes often develop a very narrow window of tolerance. Not because they are weak - please hear this - but because they learned in a world that genuinely required hypervigilance. Their nervous systems became exquisitely sensitive instruments for detecting threat. In that particular world, that sensitivity was protective. It may have kept them safe. It may have let them know when to hide, when to become invisible, when to make themselves small.

The tragedy is not that they developed these skills. The tragedy is that the skills do not know when the danger has passed. The nervous system carries its calibration into adulthood like luggage that was packed for a different trip. A raised voice in an office meeting, a door slammed down the hall, a partner who comes home in a bad mood - these things arrive in a nervous system that was trained to treat them as emergencies. And the person they belong to cannot always explain why their heart is pounding over something that, objectively, should not be that frightening. They just know it is.

This is not weakness. This is history. And understanding the difference - really understanding it, in your bones, not just as an intellectual claim - is one of the most liberating things this book can offer.

✦✦✦

I want to say something here that the research rarely says, because research speaks in averages and populations and effect sizes. It does not usually say: I know what it is like to stand very still in a room and listen to the quality of silence, trying to determine from the quality of silence alone what kind of night this is going to be. I know what it is like to become extremely good at that skill. And I know that the same skill - reading a room, scanning for subtle emotional cues, being the first to sense a shift in atmosphere - follows you everywhere. Into classrooms. Into friendships. Into workplaces. Into relationships where it has absolutely no business operating at all, except that the body does not know that yet.

If any part of that is familiar to you, I am not asking you to feel sad about it right now. I am just asking you to recognize it. To give it a name. Because things that have names are things you can eventually work with.

1.3 - The Invisible Wound: Emotional Neglect

When people think about childhood wounds, they tend to think about things that happened. Events. Incidents. The loud, dramatic, visible wrongs that leave marks everyone can see. But some of the deepest wounds in childhood are made not by what happened but by what did not. By the absence of things that should have been there. And of all the absences a child can live with, the absence of consistent, reliable, unconditional parental love is perhaps the one that reshapes the self most quietly and most thoroughly.

Emotional neglect is not always a matter of bad parents in the obvious sense. Sometimes it lives in homes that look fine from the outside. There is food. There is shelter. The bills are paid. No one is hitting anyone. But the child moves through the house like a ghost - present, unseen. Their emotional reality is not reflected back to them. When they are sad, nobody asks why. When they are proud, nobody shares the pride. When they are confused or frightened, they learn that those feelings are not welcome in the room, or that they will be dismissed, or that expressing them will cost something they cannot afford to spend.

This kind of neglect is invisible in almost every social sense. It leaves no bruises. It produces no obvious incidents to report. And yet its effects on the developing self are, research consistently shows, as significant and as lasting as more overtly traumatic forms of childhood adversity.

Bowlby, Ainsworth, and the Science of Needing to Be Seen

In the 1950s and 60s, a British psychiatrist named John Bowlby began proposing something that was, at the time, considered almost radical: that the bond between a child and their primary caregiver is not a secondary phenomenon, not merely a by-product of the fact that the caregiver provides food and warmth, but a primary biological need. As fundamental as the need to eat. As basic as the need to breathe.

Bowlby called this attachment. And his theory - developed over decades of careful observation and later supported by an enormous body of empirical research - proposed that humans are biologically wired to seek and maintain closeness to a protective figure, especially under conditions of threat or distress. The attachment system is, at its core, a survival mechanism. The infant who stays close to its caregiver survives. The infant who wanders alone in a dangerous world does not. So evolution built into us a deep, powerful, persistent need to be connected.

Mary Ainsworth, a developmental psychologist who worked with and expanded on Bowlby's ideas, designed a now-famous experiment in the 1970s called the Strange Situation. The procedure is simple: a young child and their caregiver enter an unfamiliar room. The caregiver leaves. A stranger enters. The caregiver returns. What happens in those small moments - particularly in how the child responds when the caregiver returns - turns out to be extraordinarily revealing about the quality of the attachment relationship.

Ainsworth identified three main patterns. Securely attached children, whose caregivers had been reliably responsive to their needs, were distressed when the parent left but comforted when they returned. They used the parent as a safe base from which to explore, and returned to them as a refuge when frightened. Anxiously attached children, whose caregivers had been inconsistently responsive, became highly distressed and remained difficult to soothe even after the parent's return - as if they could not trust that comfort, once offered, would last. Avoidantly attached children, whose caregivers had been consistently dismissive or unresponsive, appeared almost indifferent to the parent's absence and return - a performance of self-sufficiency that concealed, neuroimaging would later show, a masked internal stress response just as elevated as the openly distressed children.

A fourth pattern - disorganized attachment - was identified later, primarily by researcher Mary Main. This pattern, associated with caregivers who were themselves frightening or traumatized, is the one most commonly seen in children from abusive homes. The child in disorganized attachment faces an irresolvable biological dilemma: the person who is supposed to be their refuge from threat is also the source of it. The attachment system and the fear system activate simultaneously, pointing in opposite directions. And the result, in the child's behavior, is exactly what the name suggests: disorganization. Approach and avoidance at once. Confusion. Sometimes freezing. Sometimes a kind of dissociative daze.

> *The child who cannot trust the person who is supposed to protect them learns not just that this person is unsafe. They learn something far more global, and far more damaging: that safety itself is unreliable. That comfort is a trap. That needing someone is dangerous.*

What Love Looks Like When It Was Never Modeled

Here is what the absence of reliable parental love does not do: it does not simply leave a gap. A blank space where something should be. It is more active than that, more insidious. In the absence of consistent love, the child does not conclude that love is unavailable. The child concludes something about themselves. The child's brain, still building its models of the world, interprets the absence of love as data. And the model it builds from that data is: I am the kind of person who does not get loved. Or: love is something you earn, constantly, through performance and compliance. Or: love and pain are the same thing. These conclusions are not conscious. They do not arrive as thoughts. They arrive as felt truth, as the baseline assumption beneath all subsequent experience.

The philosopher and child psychoanalyst Donald Winnicott spoke of the 'good enough' mother - a caregiver who does not have to be perfect, who is simply present and responsive enough that the child develops a sense of basic trust in the world. Not trust as a philosophical position. Trust as a bodily felt sense. The knowledge, inscribed somewhere deeper than thought, that the world is navigable. That other people are, more often than not, safe. That when you need something and reach for it, the reaching is likely to be met.

When that basic trust is not established - when the reaching is met, consistently, with nothing, or with something that hurts - what develops instead is what we might call a distorted internal map of love. Not no map. A wrong one. A map that says: love is conditional. Love is scarce. Love must be constantly re-earned.

Love will abandon you. Love, if you get too close to it, will turn into something sharp.

These maps do not get filed away as memories. They get written into relationship patterns, into how we respond to intimacy, into what we expect from other people, into the story we unconsciously tell ourselves about whether we are fundamentally loveable or fundamentally, quietly, not enough.

We will spend an entire chapter later in this book on love and relationships, on the extraordinary difficulty and extraordinary possibility of learning to love differently than you were taught. But I want to name it here, early, because it is one of the most common and most silent wounds that people carry. And it is a wound that tends to compound quietly, invisibly, for decades, before a person can even find the words to describe what is wrong.

1.4 - Metaphor: The Unlit Room

I want to try to give all of this science a shape that you can feel, not just understand.

Imagine a room. It is a room that will eventually be someone's home - the core room of their inner life, the place they return to when they need to understand themselves. In the years when this room is being built and painted - the earliest years, the years before memory solidifies, the years of the highest neural plasticity - the room is lit only by whatever light the environment provides.

In a home where warmth and safety are present, the room is lit well. The painters can see what they are doing. The colors are applied with some intention, some care. There are beautiful things on the walls, and there is enough light to see them clearly.

But in a home where chaos is the weather - where the lights are off, or flickering, or sometimes so bright they hurt and sometimes completely dark - the painting goes on anyway. It always does. The brain never stops building. But it builds in the dark, from whatever materials are available, according to whatever the dim light suggests. And the colors that go on in that darkness are not necessarily the colors anyone would have chosen. They are the colors of survival. The colors of a world that made specific and often painful demands.

> *You do not get to choose what gets painted on your walls in the dark. But - and this matters enormously - you do eventually get to turn on the light. And you do eventually, with work and time and the right kind of help, get to choose what stays and what gets painted over.*

That is not a small thing. In fact, it is the whole arc of this book.

The metaphor of the unlit room is not a metaphor of doom. It is a metaphor of sequence. First comes the painting in the dark - the formation, the wounding, the construction of a self under conditions that were not chosen. Then comes the turning on of lights - the work of understanding, of looking clearly at what is actually on the walls. And then comes the most human and the most difficult part: deciding, wall by wall, what to keep and what to paint over, knowing that the painting is never quite finished, that the room keeps changing, that you yourself keep changing, and that this is not a failure of the process. It is the process.

✦✦✦

There is something I have noticed, in reading about this subject and in living inside it, that I think deserves to be said plainly before we go any further. The science of childhood adversity can sometimes feel, if you are on the receiving end of it, like a long enumeration of what was done to you. A catalogue of damage. And that is not what I want this book to be. Not because the damage is not real - it is, and we are not going to pretend otherwise - but because damage is not the whole story.

The brain that was rewired by fear is also the brain that became extraordinarily good at reading other people. The child who had to navigate emotional chaos developed, often, a depth of emotional intelligence that those raised in simpler circumstances simply do not have. The person who had to think very carefully, from a very young age, about how to survive in a complicated human environment - that person often becomes a sophisticated thinker about human nature. A writer. A scientist. A philosopher. A person who asks harder questions than most people think to ask, because they had to.

I am not saying the price was worth it. I am not that kind of optimist. The price was too high, and no child should have to pay it. But I am saying that the person on the other side of a difficult childhood is not simply a damaged version of what they might have been. They are someone different - someone who was built in specific conditions, who carries specific capacities alongside specific wounds, and who deserves to understand all of it: the science, the history, and the genuine, neuroplasticity-backed possibility of being different tomorrow than you are today.

Before We Move Forward

This chapter was always going to be the hardest one to begin. Not because the science is complicated - it is, but we have walked through it together - but because what the science is describing is personal. It is your brain. Your nervous system. Your childhood and whatever it did or did not give you.

What I hope you are taking away from these pages is not a clinical label or a tidy framework, but something simpler and more important: a sense that the patterns you live with make sense. That the way you respond to the world - the hypervigilance, the armoring, the difficulty with trust, the strange intensity of certain emotions, the numbness around others - these are not character flaws. They are not evidence that something is fundamentally wrong with you. They are the fingerprints of a particular history, left in a particular nervous system, by experiences that were real.

Understanding that is not the end of anything. It is the very beginning. The lights are coming on. Now we can see what is on the walls.

☒ *Chapter 2: The Biology of Fear*

2

The Biology of Fear

What Trauma Does to the Brain, Body, and the Very Sense of Self

"Fear is not a feeling. It is a full-body rewrite of reality."

Before we go into the science - and we will go deep into it - I want you to try something. Think about the last time you were genuinely afraid. Not the polite, manageable anxiety of a job interview or a difficult conversation. I mean real fear. The kind that arrived before you could think about it. The kind that moved through your body like a current.

Your heart accelerated. Your breathing changed - shallower, faster, almost imperceptible at first. The muscles in your shoulders and jaw tightened without you deciding to tighten them. The world outside your immediate environment - the future, yesterday's worries, the grocery list - went quiet, because your entire nervous system suddenly had a single and very urgent priority. Whatever was threatening you.

Now here is the thing I want you to understand about that experience: not one piece of it was emotional. Every single thing I just described was biological. Your body was running a program - ancient, exquisitely refined, written across millions of years of evolution - designed for one purpose: to keep you alive. Fear is not, in its origins, a psychological phenomenon. It is a physiological event. And understanding what that means, scientifically and personally, is the work of this chapter.

Because for those of us who grew up in homes where danger was not a rare emergency but a recurring weather pattern - where fear was not an occasional visitor but a climate - that program ran constantly. It shaped us at the cellular level. And the consequences of that - the ways in which chronic childhood fear reorganizes the brain, the nervous system, the immune system, the very structure of the self - are both more profound and more specific than most people realize.

Let us go through it slowly. Let us do it the way it deserves to be done - with rigor and with honesty and with the kind of respect that science, at its best, offers to human experience when it says: here is the mechanism. Here is what actually happened inside you. And here, finally, is why.

2.1 - The Amygdala: Your Brain's Alarm System

Deep inside your brain - tucked beneath the wrinkled cortex, in a region called the temporal lobe - sits a small, almond-shaped cluster of neurons. Two of them, actually, one in each hemisphere. Together they are called the amygdala, from the Greek word for almond, and they are among the most studied structures in all of neuroscience, because they sit at the center of something that turns out to matter enormously: how the brain detects and responds to threat.

The amygdala does not think. It does not reason, plan, or weigh options. What it does is pattern-match, at extraordinary speed, against a library of known or learned threats, and respond accordingly. Neuroscientist Joseph LeDoux spent decades mapping what he called 'the low road' of fear - a neural pathway that runs from the sensory thalamus directly to the amygdala, bypassing the cortex entirely. This pathway is fast. Staggeringly fast. The amygdala can initiate a fear response in as little as twelve milliseconds - before your conscious mind has had even a fraction of a second to process what it is responding to.

This is not a design flaw. It is the whole point. In the ancestral environment in which this system evolved, the cost of responding to a non-threat as if it were a threat was small - wasted energy, a moment of unnecessary alarm. The cost of not responding to a real threat as if it were a threat was death. So the amygdala is calibrated to overreact dramatically on the side of caution. It fires first, asks questions never, and leaves the cortex to sort out the aftermath.

> *Your conscious mind thinks it is driving. Your amygdala knows better. It has already slammed the brakes - or floored the accelerator - before the thinking mind has*

> *even read the road sign.*

How the Amygdala Learns to Be Afraid

The amygdala is not born knowing what to fear. It learns. Through a process called fear conditioning - studied first in rats by LeDoux and later mapped extensively in humans - the amygdala associates neutral stimuli with threatening ones. A sound that preceded something painful becomes, through repeated pairing, a sound that triggers the fear response on its own. This is what Ivan Pavlov was discovering with his dogs, though he did not have the neural vocabulary to describe it in those terms. The brain learns what predicts danger, and it learns it fast and it learns it deep.

In a child raised in a dangerous or unpredictable home, the amygdala's fear library gets built from a specific and often painful curriculum. The particular sound of a car pulling into the driveway. The specific quality of silence that means something is wrong. A tone of voice. A smell. A posture. The way someone moves when they are about to become threatening. These associations get encoded in the amygdala with the same efficiency and the same permanence as any other survival-critical learning, because from the brain's evolutionary perspective, that is precisely what they are.

The problem - and it is a problem that will ripple outward through every domain of adult life - is that fear conditioning is remarkably durable and remarkably non-specific. The amygdala does not only respond to the original threatening stimulus. It generalizes. It responds to things that resemble the original threat. To contexts that share features with the context in which the threat occurred. This is adaptive when the generalization is accurate - if a particular species of snake hurt you, being wary of similar-looking snakes makes sense. But when the generalization is based on a childhood environment, it can turn ordinary adult life into a minefield of false alarms.

The adult who flinches when someone raises their voice - even in laughter. Who feels their heart rate spike at the sound of glass breaking, even in a kitchen. Who becomes paralyzed with anxiety in situations that are, by any rational measure, safe. Who reads threat into neutral facial expressions, into ambiguous tones of voice, into the body language of people who mean no harm. These are not irrational responses. They are the amygdala doing exactly what it was trained to do, running the program it was given, in a world where that program no longer fits. The alarm is not broken. It was calibrated for a different building.

> *Research note: Neuroimaging studies consistently show heightened amygdala reactivity in adults with histories of childhood maltreatment, even in the absence of current threat. A 2011 study by McCrory and colleagues found that abused children showed greater amygdala activation in response to angry faces than non-abused children - suggesting that threat-detection systems become biased toward threat detection in environments where threats were common. The amygdala did not*

> *malfunction. It learned.*

Extinction and Why Fear Is So Hard to Unlearn

Here is something the research on fear conditioning reveals that is both discouraging and important to understand: fear extinction - the process by which the brain learns that a previously threatening stimulus is no longer dangerous - is not the same as forgetting. When a conditioned fear response is extinguished, the original fear memory is not erased. A new memory is created, layered over the old one, that says: this thing is now safe. But the original memory persists. And under conditions of stress, or fatigue, or contexts that resemble the original threat environment, the old memory can re-emerge. Scientists call this spontaneous recovery. The fear comes back.

This has enormous practical implications for people working through childhood trauma. The progress is real, and it is hard-won, and it is neurologically genuine. But it is not linear. There will be moments - sometimes years into recovery, sometimes decades - when an old fear comes flooding back with the freshness of something that just happened, triggered by a context or a sensory detail that the conscious mind does not even register as significant. This is not regression. It is not evidence that the work was wasted. It is the architecture of fear memory being what it is: layered, durable, and sensitive to context in ways that can catch even experienced therapists off guard.

2.2 - Cortisol, ACEs, and the Body That Keeps the Score

In 1995 - the year I was born - a physician named Vincent Felitti made an accidental discovery that would change the field of public health. Felitti was running an obesity clinic in San Diego and was puzzled by a paradox: his most successful patients - those who lost the most weight - were also the ones most likely to drop out of the program. They were not failing to lose weight. They were succeeding, and then fleeing.

When he began interviewing these patients, he discovered something he had not expected. A significant number of them had histories of childhood sexual abuse. And as he probed further, he found that the weight - often gained rapidly after a period of thinness - seemed to be functioning as something. As protection. As insulation. As a body's way of saying: I need to be less visible. I need to be less attractive. I need to be safe in a way that nothing external has made me feel safe.

Felitti partnered with epidemiologist Robert Anda at the Centers for Disease Control, and together they launched what became the ACE Study - the Adverse Childhood Experiences Study - one of the largest and most consequential investigations of its kind ever conducted. Between 1995 and 1997, they surveyed over seventeen thousand patients of the Kaiser Permanente health system in California, asking about ten categories of childhood adversity: physical, emotional, and sexual abuse; physical and emotional neglect; and five categories of household dysfunction including witnessing domestic violence, living with a substance-abusing family member, having an incarcerated family member, losing a parent through divorce or abandonment, and living with a mentally ill family member.

Each category counted as one point in an ACE score. And what they found when they correlated ACE scores with health outcomes was, even for researchers who expected a relationship, staggering.

> *Childhood adversity was not merely associated with psychological problems in adulthood. It was associated with heart disease. With cancer. With chronic lung disease. With liver disease. With autoimmune conditions. With obesity. With addiction. With shortened life expectancy. The body was keeping a record of what happened to the mind - and eventually presenting the bill.*

The Numbers That Changed Everything

The ACE Study's findings are worth sitting with, because they resist the instinct to minimize them. Adults with an ACE score of four or more - meaning four or more categories of childhood adversity - were twice as likely to be smokers, seven times more likely to be alcoholic, and ten times more likely to have injected street drugs compared to those with an ACE score of zero. They had a thirty percent higher risk of heart disease, a two hundred percent higher risk of liver disease, and a four hundred sixty percent increase in depression.

And perhaps most arresting of all: adults with ACE scores of six or higher had a lifespan, on average, twenty years shorter than those with a score of zero. Twenty years. Not a statistical quirk. Twenty years of actual human life, gone, traceable in a direct and measurable line back to what happened in childhood.

The mechanism at the center of much of this is the stress-response system we introduced in Chapter 1 - specifically, the chronic overactivation of the HPA axis and the hormone it produces: cortisol.

What Cortisol Does When It Never Goes Away

Cortisol is not a villain. In the right amount, at the right time, cortisol is essential. It mobilizes energy. It enhances certain types of memory - particularly memory for emotionally significant events, which is why you remember clearly where you were on the day something terrible happened. It modulates immune function. It regulates the sleep-wake cycle. Cortisol is doing important work, constantly.

But chronic cortisol - the cortisol of an HPA axis that has been activated so repeatedly, for so long, in a body that has never been allowed to fully return to baseline - is a different thing. It becomes corrosive. And its targets in a developing child's body are numerous and specific.

The hippocampus, as we touched on in Chapter 1, is particularly vulnerable. It is dense with cortisol receptors, and chronic cortisol exposure literally shrinks it - reducing the number of neurons, suppressing neurogenesis, disrupting the synaptic connections that allow it to do its jobs: forming explicit memories, regulating the stress response itself, and putting experience into temporal and contextual perspective. A damaged hippocampus cannot regulate the HPA axis effectively, which means the stress system stays activated longer in response to stressors, which means more cortisol, which means more hippocampal damage. The system feeds on itself.

In the prefrontal cortex - the region responsible for executive function, for impulse control, for the capacity to think before you act and to regulate emotion through reason - chronic cortisol similarly disrupts development and function. The prefrontal cortex is the last region of the brain to fully mature, not completing its development until the mid-twenties. In a child whose cortisol system is chronically elevated, this protracted development occurs in a neurochemical environment that makes it harder for the prefrontal cortex to establish the kind of robust, reliable connections that eventually allow a person to manage strong emotions without being overwhelmed by them.

> *Research note: A landmark 2012 study by Teicher and Samson found that childhood maltreatment was associated with reduced grey matter volume in the prefrontal cortex, the hippocampus, and the corpus callosum, with effects varying by the type of maltreatment and the developmental period during which it occurred. Critically, these were not fixed deficits - neuroplasticity research suggests many of these changes can be at least*

> *partially reversed through appropriate intervention. The brain that was shaped by chronic stress can be reshaped. But first, it has to be understood.*

The Immune System and Inflammation: When the Body Declares War on Itself

There is a dimension of the ACE research that gets less popular attention but is, scientifically, among the most important: the relationship between childhood adversity and systemic inflammation. Because chronic psychological stress - the kind produced by living in a dangerous or emotionally depriving environment - does not stay in the brain. It travels.

The nervous system, the endocrine system, and the immune system are in constant communication. Psychoneuroimmunology - a field that has exploded in the last two decades - studies exactly this: how psychological experience gets translated into immune function, and vice versa. What it has found, consistently, is that chronic stress produces a state of low-grade systemic inflammation - elevated levels of pro-inflammatory cytokines like interleukin-6 and tumor necrosis factor - that, sustained over time, underlies a remarkable number of adult diseases.

This is one of the pathways through which childhood adversity produces adult cardiovascular disease, autoimmune conditions, and accelerated cellular aging. Researchers have found that adults with high ACE scores show measurable changes in telomere length - the protective caps on chromosomes that shorten with age and with cellular stress. Shortened telomeres are a biomarker of accelerated biological aging. The person with a high ACE score may not only feel older than their chronological age. They may, at the cellular level, actually be.

I want to be precise here about what this means and what it does not mean. It does not mean that a difficult childhood sentences a person to disease. It does not mean the outcome is fixed or that the body cannot recover. What it means is that the relationship between psychological experience and physical health is not metaphorical, not merely correlational, but mechanistic. The body is not separate from the story. It is part of the story. And any account of childhood trauma that does not account for the body is an incomplete account.

2.3 - The Prefrontal Cortex Goes Offline

Let me describe a scenario that will be familiar, in some version, to almost anyone who grew up in a chaotic or threatening home.

You are in a conversation. Everything is fine - or at least, everything appears fine by the objective measures available to an outside observer. And then something happens. A particular word. A change in tone. A look. A silence. Something small, something that a person with a different history might not even register. And suddenly you are not in the conversation anymore. Or rather, your body is there, but something has shifted. The room seems different. Your heart is moving faster. Your thoughts are either racing or gone completely. You say something you did not intend to say. Or you go silent when you meant to speak. Or you feel a wash of emotion that is disproportionate - that you can see is disproportionate, from some distant observational post - but that you cannot seem to modulate.

What happened? In neurological terms: your prefrontal cortex went offline.

Under conditions of acute stress or perceived threat, the brain undergoes a rapid shift in resource allocation. The amygdala's alarm, once triggered, initiates a cascade that effectively deprioritizes the prefrontal cortex. Blood flow shifts. Norepinephrine floods the system. The prefrontal cortex - which is metabolically expensive, slow by the standards of threat-response, and frankly unnecessary for the immediate business of survival - loses its regulatory grip on behavior and emotion. What takes over is faster, older, and less sophisticated: the limbic system, the brainstem, the survival circuitry that was running the show long before the cortex showed up in evolutionary history.

> *This is why people say and do things under stress that they would never say or do in calm reflection. The calm, reflective self is the cortex. And the cortex does not get a vote when the amygdala has decided this is an emergency.*

The Thinking Brain and the Survival Brain

Daniel Siegel, the interpersonal neurobiologist whose work has done perhaps more than anyone else's to translate complex neuroscience into humanly useful frameworks, offers a simple but powerful metaphor. He describes the brain as a hand. Fold your fingers over your thumb, and you have roughly the architecture of the human brain: the brainstem and limbic system are the thumb and palm, responsible for survival functions, emotion, and basic regulatory processes; the cortex is the fingers, folded over the top, capable of higher-order cognition, language, and emotional regulation.

When the alarm goes off - when the amygdala fires and the stress cascade begins - the fingers fly open. The cortex comes offline. Siegel calls this 'flipping the lid.' And anyone who has experienced it - who has watched themselves behave in ways they cannot quite account for during moments of high stress - knows exactly what it feels like from the inside. The lid flips, and something older and less careful takes the wheel.

For children raised in environments of chronic threat, the lid was flipping constantly. Not as an occasional emergency response, but as a near-daily event. And because the prefrontal cortex develops through use - because its neural pathways are strengthened through practice, through thousands of moments of exercising regulation, reflection, and response-inhibition - a childhood spent in survival mode is a childhood in which that practice was not happening. The cortex was offline too often to get properly online.

This is not a character flaw in the adult who struggles with impulse control, emotional flooding, or the capacity to think clearly under pressure. It is the entirely predictable outcome of a brain that was shaped by a particular set of experiences. The part of you that would have learned to regulate, to pause, to reflect - it was busy with something else. It was busy surviving.

Executive Function and the Compound Interest of Chaos

Executive function is the umbrella term for the cognitive capacities managed primarily by the prefrontal cortex: working memory, cognitive flexibility, planning, inhibitory control, attention regulation. These are the capacities that allow a person to hold a goal in mind while resisting distraction, to shift strategies when one approach is not working, to stop themselves from saying the thing they will regret, to manage the demands of the present without losing sight of the future.

Research consistently shows that children who have experienced significant adversity demonstrate measurable differences in executive function compared to their peers. Not because they are less intelligent - adversity has no particular relationship with raw cognitive capacity - but because the neural infrastructure of executive function was developing in a brain that was frequently in threat-response mode, flooded with cortisol, and deprived of the conditions under which executive function develops best: safety, predictability, and the gentle, repeated practice of regulation supported by an attuned caregiver.

And here is where it compounds. Executive function is not

merely one thing among many. It is the metacognitive foundation from which everything else is built. Learning in school requires executive function. Maintaining relationships requires it. Managing a job, handling money, navigating bureaucracy, planning a future - all of it sits on the foundation of executive function. When that foundation is shaky, not because of any inherent deficiency but because it was built under difficult conditions, the effects ripple outward across every domain of a person's life. This is part of why the ACE research finds such sweeping correlations across such apparently unrelated outcomes. The common thread is not one specific symptom. It is the foundational cognitive and emotional infrastructure - the executive function, the stress-regulation system, the capacity for trust and connection - that was shaped by early adversity and that shapes everything downstream.

I want to sit here for a moment and say something that the clinical literature sometimes forgets to say, because clinical literature is not always written by people who have sat on the other side of the desk.

When you read about these effects - the hippocampal shrinkage, the amygdala hyper-reactivity, the prefrontal cortex going offline, the executive function deficits - there is a way that it can feel like being told your brain is broken. Like being given a diagnosis that explains everything while somehow making it worse. Like the science is closing a door instead of opening one.

I want to be very clear: that is not what the science is saying. What the science is saying is something far more nuanced and far more hopeful. It is saying: your brain is not broken. Your brain adapted. Your brain did what every brain does - it learned. It built itself around the specific demands of the specific world it grew up in. And because the brain is not a static organ - because neuroplasticity is not a metaphor but a biological reality that persists, to varying degrees, throughout the human lifespan - the fact that it adapted once means it is capable of adapting again. The shape of the present is not the permanent shape of the future.

We will come back to this, extensively, in Part Three of this book. For now, I want to hold both things at once: the genuine weight of what chronic childhood fear does to a developing brain and body, and the equally genuine truth that this is not the end of the story. It is the beginning of the story. A beginning that some people were handed without being asked, and that most of them have spent their lives trying to understand.

2.4 - Sexual Trauma: A Body That Remembers What the Mind Tries to Forget

There is a particular kind of wound that deserves its own conversation, because its biology is specific and its aftermath is frequently misunderstood and because the silence around it - the silence that has historically surrounded childhood sexual abuse - has done almost as much damage as the abuse itself.

Childhood sexual abuse is, among the forms of childhood adversity, one of the most prevalent and one of the most studied, precisely because its effects are so pervasive and so lasting. Estimates of prevalence vary depending on methodology and population, but they consistently suggest that childhood sexual abuse affects somewhere between fifteen and thirty percent of the population - disproportionately, though not exclusively, girls, and disproportionately, though not exclusively, perpetrated by someone known and trusted by the child.

This last fact - that the perpetrator is usually known, usually trusted, often loved - is neurologically significant. It is not just an aggravating factor in the moral sense. It creates a specific and brutal neurological predicament, one that overlaps with what we discussed in Chapter 1 about disorganized attachment: the person who is causing harm is also the person to whom the child is biologically driven to turn for safety and comfort. The attachment system and the threat system are simultaneously activated, pointing in opposite directions. The result, in the brain and nervous system of the child, is a kind of biological civil war.

Dissociation: The Emergency Exit the Brain Builds for Itself

When experience becomes unbearable - when what is happening is too frightening, too painful, too incoherent to be processed in the normal way - the brain sometimes does something extraordinary. It disconnects. Not completely, not literally, but functionally: it creates a kind of internal distance from the experience, a dissociation between what is happening to the body and what the conscious mind is registering. The experience still occurs. It is still encoded. But it is encoded differently - in fragments, in images, in body sensations rather than coherent narrative, in a form that the ordinary memory system cannot retrieve in the ordinary way.

Dissociation exists on a spectrum. At the mild end, it is entirely ordinary - the highway hypnosis of a long drive you cannot remember, the daydream in a lecture that swallows twenty minutes whole. At the more severe end, it can involve depersonalization - the sense of watching yourself from outside your body, of being a spectator in your own life - or derealization, the sense that the world around you is not quite real, that there is a sheet of glass between you and everything else. It can involve amnesia for specific events or periods of time. It can, in its most severe form, involve the kind of fragmented self-states that have historically been described as dissociative identity disorder.

All of these, across the spectrum, represent the same fundamental mechanism: a brain using the resources available to it to survive an experience it cannot otherwise survive intact. Dissociation is not a malfunction. It is emergency architecture. A firewall. A mind protecting itself the only way it knows how.

> *The body remembers what the mind cannot afford to. That is not a poetic claim. It is a neurological description of how trauma memory works - stored in sensation, in posture, in the startle of a smell, in the body's insistence on reactions the conscious mind cannot explain and did not choose.*

Trauma Memory and the Body's Archive

Bessel van der Kolk, the Dutch-American psychiatrist whose book 'The Body Keeps the Score' has reached more readers than almost any other work of trauma neuroscience, articulates a principle that is central to understanding childhood sexual abuse and its aftermath: traumatic memory is not stored the way ordinary memory is stored. Ordinary memory is reconstructive - a narrative assembled from fragments, shaped by subsequent experience, subject to the normal processes of memory consolidation and revision. Traumatic memory, by contrast, tends to be stored in its original sensory form. Raw. Unprocessed. In the amygdala rather than the hippocampus. Unassimilated into the coherent story of a life.

This is why trauma survivors often describe being 'triggered' - a word that has been somewhat diluted by cultural overuse, but that describes a genuine and specific neurological event. A sensory input - a smell, a sound, a touch, a particular quality of light or pressure or movement - arrives at the nervous system and activates, directly and without narrative mediation, the stored sensory memory of the original trauma. The body responds as if the trauma is happening now, because in the amygdala's timeless archive, it is. The prefrontal cortex may know perfectly well that this is the year it is, that the person in front of you is not who hurt you, that you are safe. But the body does not experience it that way. The body is still in that room.

For those who experienced sexual abuse in childhood, this can manifest in ways that are confusing, sometimes terrifying, and often accompanied by profound shame - as if the reactions are evidence of weakness or pathology rather than what they actually are: the predictable neurological aftermath of an experience the nervous system was never equipped to process at the time it occurred. Hyperarousal at unexpected moments. Numbness where there should be sensation, and sensation where there should be numbness. Complicated, sometimes seemingly contradictory relationships with the body - with physicality, with intimacy, with the simple act of inhabiting a self that was violated.

These are not character flaws. They are not evidence of being broken. They are the body's archive, speaking in the only language it has: sensation, response, the insistence of memory that was never given a proper place to live.

The Silence That Compounds the Wound

There is a dimension of childhood sexual abuse that is not strictly neurological but that interacts with the neurology in ways that are important to name. That is the silence. The not-telling, which is almost universal. The vast majority of children who experience sexual abuse do not disclose it - not at the time, often not for years or decades, sometimes never. And the reasons for this silence are themselves a testimony to the cruelty of the situation: shame, fear, love for the perpetrator, the impossibility of finding language for something that was learned before language, the knowledge - instinctive, correct - that disclosure would not be believed, or would be disbelieved, or would bring consequences that feel worse than the silence.

What the silence does, neurologically, is prevent processing. The hippocampus consolidates memory partly through language - through narrative, through the act of telling a story that places events in sequence, in context, in the past. When there is no telling - when the experience lives only in the body's sensory archive, never converted into words, never placed in the context of a self that continues forward - it stays raw. It stays present tense. The silence does not protect. It preserves the wound in amber.

This is one of the most important arguments for therapy - particularly for trauma-focused therapies that specifically address this conversion of implicit, bodily, sensory memory into explicit, narrative, contextual memory. Not because talking about it makes it not have happened. But because putting the experience into language, into sequence, into the past tense where it belongs, is part of what moves it from a wound that is still bleeding into a wound that is healing. The body needs the story to stop treating the past as the present.

✦✦✦

I want to close this section by saying something that should not need saying but apparently does, because the world in which we live has made it necessary: none of what happened to children who were sexually abused was their fault. In any form, in any circumstance, under any framing that the perpetrator or the culture or the internalized voice of shame might offer.

Children do not have the neurological, psychological, or social development to consent to sexual experience with adults. Their brains are literally not capable of it - the prefrontal cortex, which governs the kind of autonomous, informed, context-understanding decision-making that consent requires, is decades from completion. The child who did not fight back was not consenting. The child who did not tell was not consenting. The child who experienced confusion, or physical sensation, or attachment to the person who hurt them - none of these are evidence of consent. They are evidence of a child's brain responding the way a child's brain responds: with the resources it has, under the conditions it was given, doing the best it could.

The shame belongs to no one in this story but the person who chose to cause harm. Not to the child who survived it. And not to the adult who is still carrying it.

What We Now Know - and What It Asks of Us

We have covered a lot of ground in this chapter. The amygdala and its ancient, fast, pattern-matching fear response. The HPA axis and what chronic cortisol does to a developing hippocampus, a prefrontal cortex, an immune system. The ACE Study and its sobering documentation of the physical as well as psychological costs of childhood adversity. The prefrontal cortex going offline under stress, and what that means for a childhood spent in survival mode. Sexual trauma and the particular neurology of a body that remembers what the mind tried to forget.

All of this is heavy material. I know it is. And I want to acknowledge something that might be arising in you as you read it, if you are reading it from the inside of a difficult history: the strange, complicated feeling of seeing yourself described in a scientific framework. Of having things that felt like private failure, private weakness, private confusion - things that lived in the dark, unnamed - suddenly named. Explained. Situated in a mechanism rather than in a character flaw.

That feeling - of being explained - can be complicated. It can be a relief and a grief at once. A relief because the explanation removes the shame that was sitting on something that was never about weakness. A grief because understanding why something happened does not undo the fact that it happened. The science does not go back and change the childhood. It only changes the way you understand it.

But changing the way you understand it matters. It matters because shame is one of the most powerful forces preventing healing, and because shame lives in the dark, in the unnamed, in the place where we believe that what happened to us is evidence of what we are. When the light comes on - when the mechanism is visible - the shame has nowhere to hide. It was never about what you are. It was always about what happened to you. And what happened to you was biology, doing what biology does in the face of conditions it was not built to withstand indefinitely.

You were not built wrong. You were built in a difficult place. That is the conclusion of Chapter 2 - and it is the foundation on which everything that follows will stand.

☒ *Chapter 3: What We Learn Before We Can Think*

3

What We Learn Before We Can Think

Attachment, Bonding, and the Templates We Carry

"The first love story you ever lived is the one you keep trying to rewrite."

Think about the last time you walked into a new relationship - a friendship, a romance, a new job with a new boss - and felt, almost immediately, like you already knew how it was going to go. Not because you had information. Just a feeling. A hunch that settled into your chest before you had any real evidence to support it.

Maybe you felt certain this person would eventually leave. Or that if you asked for too much, they would stop liking you. Or that you needed to be useful, entertaining, low-maintenance - that your bare, unperforming self was not quite enough. Or maybe the opposite: you felt, unusually, a warmth and ease that surprised you, a sense that this person was safe in a way you could not quite explain.

Where does that come from? That immediate, wordless, below-the-surface knowing about how a relationship is going to feel?

It comes from something that was written into you before you had language. Before you had memories you can access. Before you had any conscious idea that learning was even happening. It comes from the very first relationship you ever had - the one with the person who held you, or did not hold you, who looked at you, or looked through you, who came when you cried, or did not come. The relationship that taught your nervous system what to expect from other human beings. What they are like. Whether they can be trusted. Whether you, yourself, are worth being close to.

This is what attachment theory is about. And it is one of the most important ideas in all of psychology - not because it is complicated, but because it is so simple, and so early, and so lasting.

3.1 - Bowlby, Ainsworth, and the Science of Bonding

John Bowlby was a British psychiatrist who spent years working with troubled and delinquent children in the 1940s. And he noticed something that seems obvious once you hear it, but that the psychological establishment of his time actively resisted: children who had been separated from their mothers, or who had never formed a stable bond with a caregiver, were consistently more troubled, more anxious, more prone to emotional and behavioral difficulties than those who had.

This seems obvious to us now. But the dominant view in Bowlby's era was something quite different. The prevailing theory - rooted partly in behaviorism, partly in a certain cultural stoicism about child-rearing - was that children attached to their mothers primarily because mothers provided food. Love was secondary. Connection was a bonus. What mattered was feeding and warmth and physical care. The emotional bond itself was, in this view, not particularly important.

Bowlby thought that was completely wrong. And he had the evidence to show it. He pointed to studies of children raised in institutions - orphanages, hospitals - who were fed adequately, kept clean and warm, but had no consistent caregiver to form a bond with. These children, despite adequate physical care, showed profound disturbances: developmental delays, emotional flatness, an inability to form relationships, in some cases complete withdrawal from the world. Some of them died, despite adequate nutrition, from what researchers at the time called marasmus - a wasting away that seemed to have no physical cause. They died, as one researcher put it, from lack of love.

Bowlby argued that the need for attachment - for a close, consistent, responsive bond with a caregiver - is not a secondary desire. It is a primary biological drive, as fundamental as hunger or thirst. Evolution built it into us because, for a helpless infant in the ancestral environment, proximity to a protective adult was literally the difference between life and death. The infant that cried when separated, that smiled to elicit closeness, that clung when frightened - that infant survived. The infant that did not signal its need for connection, that did not protest separation, that did not seek comfort - that infant was more likely to die alone.

So the attachment system is, at its root, a survival system. It is the biological drive to stay close to the people who keep us safe. And it is exquisitely sensitive - especially in the earliest years - to whether the people we are trying to stay close to are actually responsive. Whether they are there. Whether they come when we need them. Whether we can count on them.

Mary Ainsworth and the Strange Situation

In the 1970s, a developmental psychologist named Mary Ainsworth designed an experiment that was elegantly simple and produced results that changed the field. She called it the Strange Situation.

Here is how it worked. A mother and her young child - usually between twelve and eighteen months old - enter an unfamiliar room together. There are toys. The child explores. Then a stranger enters. Then the mother leaves the child alone with the stranger. Then the mother returns. And then, crucially, the researchers watch what happens next.

What they found was that children responded to this sequence in very different ways. And those different ways fell into recognizable patterns.

Some children were upset when their mother left - they cried, they searched, they clearly wanted her back. But when she returned, they went to her, let themselves be comforted, calmed down, and went back to playing. These children had what Ainsworth called secure attachment. Their mother was a safe base. They trusted that she would come back. When she did, they let her in. Crisis over, back to life.

Other children were extremely distressed when their mother left - more distressed than the first group, sometimes inconsolably so. But here is the interesting part: when their mother returned, they could not be comforted. They clung and pushed away at the same time. They were angry. They could not settle. Ainsworth called this anxious-ambivalent attachment. These were children whose caregivers had been inconsistent - sometimes warm and responsive, sometimes not - so the children had learned that you could not count on comfort being available. The alarm, once triggered, could not be turned off, because turning it off would require trusting that the comfort was real and would last. And they had learned it might not.

Still other children seemed barely to react when their mother left. When she returned, they turned away, went back to their toys, seemed almost indifferent. Avoidant attachment, Ainsworth called it. But here is what neuroimaging later revealed: these children were not actually calm. Their heart rates and cortisol levels were just as elevated as the distressed children. They had simply learned to suppress the outward display of distress - because their caregivers had been consistently unresponsive to emotional expression, they had learned, very early, that showing need did not help. So they stopped showing it. The need remained. It just went underground.

> *Avoidant attachment is not indifference. It is pain that learned not to show its face, because showing its face never brought anyone closer.*

The Fourth Pattern: When Love and Fear Share the Same Face

Ainsworth's three categories held for several decades. Then a researcher named Mary Main added a fourth. She called it disorganized attachment, and it is the one most commonly found in children who grew up in abusive or severely neglectful homes.

These children, in the Strange Situation, showed behavior that did not fit any pattern. They would approach their caregiver and then suddenly freeze. Or they would turn toward the caregiver and then veer away at the last moment. Or they would look frightened by the very person who was supposed to be their comfort. Their behavior seemed contradictory, disorganized - and it was, because the situation they were in was biologically contradictory.

Think about what it means when the person who hurts you is also the person you are biologically wired to run to when you are hurt. When the source of the threat and the source of the comfort are the same person. Your attachment system says: go to them, they are your safe person. Your threat system says: stay away, they are dangerous. Both systems fire simultaneously, each pulling in the opposite direction, and the result is a kind of neurological paralysis. The child cannot resolve the dilemma because the dilemma is unresolvable.

Disorganized attachment has the strongest association with later psychological difficulties of any of the four patterns. Not because the children who develop it are weaker or less capable - they are not - but because the core organizing principle of their attachment system is chaos. Their internal model of relationships was built from the experience that closeness is both necessary and dangerous, that the people you need most are the people most likely to harm you. That model does not simply disappear when childhood ends. It travels.

3.2 - Disorganized Attachment: When the Safe Person Is Also the Scary One

I want to stay with disorganized attachment a little longer, because I think it is the pattern that is most poorly understood - and most poorly understood in ways that do real harm to people who carry it.

Here is what disorganized attachment looks like in adulthood, because it does not announce itself the way it did in infancy. It does not look like a child freezing in a doorway. It looks like this:

> *You meet someone who feels safe. And that feeling of safety - that warmth, that ease - immediately makes you suspicious. You start looking for the catch. You pull back just as the closeness increases. Or you find yourself*

simultaneously desperate for connection and terrified of it, both feelings present at once, each one undermining the other. Or you fall hard and fast for someone and then, when they actually become available, you find yourself strangely uninterested. Or you stay in relationships that hurt you because at least the hurt is familiar, and familiar - even when it is painful - feels safer than the unknown of something that might actually be kind.

None of this is chosen. None of it is a personality trait. It is a nervous system doing what it learned to do, running the program it was given in the earliest years of life. A program that was written in a world where closeness was dangerous, where the people you needed most could not be trusted, where safety and threat wore the same face.

The Internal Working Model: The Map You Carry Everywhere

Bowlby had a concept he called the internal working model. It is a simple idea with enormous implications. He proposed that, based on early attachment experiences, children construct a kind of mental model of the world - specifically, a model of how relationships work. How available and responsive other people are likely to be. How worthy of care and attention the self is. What to expect when you are vulnerable. What to do when you need something.

This internal working model is not a conscious belief. It is not something a person decides. It is a set of deeply embedded expectations, encoded in the attachment system, that operate below the level of deliberate thought. It is why you can know, intellectually, that your partner is trustworthy, and still feel the anxiety that says they are about to leave. It is why you can recognize, as an adult, that asking for help is reasonable, and still feel the shame that says needing anything makes you a burden. The knowledge and the felt reality run on different tracks. The internal working model runs on a deeper track than the rational mind.

And here is the thing about internal working models: they are self-confirming. They shape behavior in ways that tend to produce the outcomes they predict. The anxiously attached person who is desperate for reassurance often drives partners away with the intensity of that need - confirming the model that says people will leave. The avoidant person who cannot let others get close often ends up in relationships that stay superficial - confirming the model that says real intimacy is not possible. The model was built from experience. And then it goes on building experience in its own image.

> *The internal working model is not just a belief about the world. It is a self-fulfilling prophecy. It shapes how you act, and how you act shapes what happens, and what happens confirms what you already believed. The loop is quiet, and it is relentless.*

Why This Is Not Your Fault - And Why That Matters

I want to say something here that is both scientifically true and personally important.

The internal working model you carry - whatever shape it takes, however it has complicated your relationships and your sense of self - was not chosen. It was not a decision. It was built, piece by piece, interaction by interaction, in the years before you had any capacity to evaluate what was being built. You had no say in the curriculum. You did not get to review the lesson plan. You were simply in a particular environment, with a particular nervous system in a particular developmental window, and that environment wrote itself into you.

This matters enormously for something we will talk about throughout this book: shame. Because one of the most common and most damaging experiences for people with insecure attachment histories is the shame that comes from recognizing their own patterns. The shame of knowing that they push people away, or cling too hard, or cannot trust someone who has given them no real reason not to trust. The feeling that there is something fundamentally wrong with them, something broken in the mechanism, something that makes them unfit for the ordinary business of human connection.

The science says otherwise. The science says the mechanism is not broken. The mechanism was built for a specific environment and is running exactly as it was designed to run. The problem is that the environment changed - but the mechanism did not get the update. The map was drawn for a country that no longer exists. And the person holding it is not stupid or damaged. They are simply using the only map they were ever given.

3.3 - Love Without Template: What Happens When No Model Exists

Here is a question I find myself returning to, over and over.

If you grow up without being loved consistently - really loved, in the full sense of being seen and held and valued and responded to - how do you know what love is? How do you recognize it when it shows up? How do you give it to someone else when you were never given a model of what it looks like in practice?

Most people who grew up in loving homes never have to think about this. They absorbed a model of love the same way they absorbed language - through immersion, through thousands of repeated interactions, through a kind of relational osmosis that happened before they were aware of it. They know what love feels like in their bodies, because they have felt it. They know what it looks like when someone shows up for you, because someone showed up for them. They have a template. They can recognize the real thing because they have handled it before.

But what about the person who did not have that? What does love feel like to someone whose experience of it was conditional, or intermittent, or absent, or wrapped in harm?

What do they do when they encounter something that might be genuine care - how do they evaluate it, how do they trust it, how do they let it in without the felt sense that their body knows this, that this is familiar in the good way?

What often happens is that they trust the familiar over the genuinely safe. Because familiar feels like home, even when home was not a good place. The anxious feeling of waiting to be abandoned feels more trustworthy than the unusual quiet of someone who actually stays. The intensity of a chaotic relationship feels more like love than the steadiness of someone who is simply and consistently there. Intensity was what love felt like. Steadiness feels like absence.

> *There is a particular loneliness in this. In sitting across from someone who is genuinely kind, who wants nothing from you that costs too much, who is simply - and this is the strange, almost suspicious word - available. And feeling, underneath the gratitude, a low hum of mistrust. Waiting for the catch. Waiting for the other shoe. Because in the world where your nervous system was trained, there was always another shoe.*

This is not a flaw in the person. It is the entirely predictable experience of someone whose internal working model was built on scarcity. Who learned that love has conditions, or that it is unreliable, or that it comes paired with something sharp. The template is not absent, exactly. It is wrong. And using a wrong template in a world that sometimes offers the real thing is a particular kind of suffering - to be close to what you need and unable to trust that it is actually there.

The Hunger That Does Not Know Its Own Name

There is another dimension of growing up without adequate love that I think deserves to be named, because it is common and rarely spoken about clearly.

When a child does not receive the emotional attunement and love they need, they do not simply accept the deprivation and move on. They hunger. They keep hungering, often without knowing what exactly they are hungry for. The need does not go away simply because it was not met. It transforms. It goes underground. It finds other expressions.

Sometimes it becomes an insatiable need for achievement - the belief that if you can just become good enough, accomplished enough, impressive enough, the love that was withheld will finally arrive. Sometimes it becomes a compulsive caretaking of others - pouring into everyone else the love you never received, in the unconscious hope that loving others will somehow fill what is empty in you. Sometimes it becomes addiction - to substances, to work, to intensity in relationships - because the nervous system that was never properly soothed by a caregiver is always seeking something to do that job.

None of these are moral failures. They are adaptations. The hunger is real. The need is real. And it deserves to be recognized as real - not pathologized, not shamed, but seen for what it is: the entirely human consequence of having needed something essential and not received it.

3.4 - The Neuroscience of Trust

Let us talk about trust for a moment. Not trust as a philosophical concept or a character virtue - but trust as a biological prediction. Because that is what it actually is, at the level of the nervous system.

When you trust someone, what is happening in your brain is this: your predictive system - the same system we discussed in Chapter 1, the one that is always modeling what is going to happen next - has generated a prediction that this person is safe. That they will behave in a way that does not threaten your wellbeing. That the closeness they are offering will not become a weapon. That you can lower your guard without being harmed in the moment of lowering it.

That prediction is not made from nothing. It is made from data. From pattern. From what you have learned, across a lifetime of experience - and particularly across the earliest years of that lifetime - about how people behave. And for someone whose earliest data about human beings was that they are unpredictable, or that they harm, or that they disappear when you need them most - the prediction is going to reflect that data. Not because the person is wrong to be suspicious, but because the prediction engine is working with the information it has.

Oxytocin: The Trust Chemical That Needs a Safe World to Work

You have probably heard of oxytocin. It is sometimes called the bonding hormone, or the love hormone, and it has a somewhat oversimplified reputation in popular science as the chemical that makes you trust and connect and feel warm toward other people.

The reality is more interesting. Oxytocin is not simply a trust switch. It is a social salience enhancer - it makes social information more vivid, more emotionally significant, more impactful. And here is the critical nuance: in a safe context, with a trustworthy other, it produces the warmth and connection and prosocial feelings we associate with bonding. But in an unsafe context - with an untrustworthy or threatening other - oxytocin can actually intensify feelings of anxiety and suspicion. It amplifies whatever the social context is producing. It turns up the volume.

What this means for people with early attachment wounds is significant. The system that is supposed to facilitate trust and connection - the oxytocin system - is working differently in a nervous system shaped by environments where closeness was dangerous. The same chemical that enables bonding can, in that context, sharpen the alarm. It is not that the bonding system is absent or broken. It is that it is operating in a nervous system calibrated for a world where trusting was a risk, and it reflects that calibration.

> *Trust is not a decision you make with your mind. It is a prediction your nervous system makes with your history. And for people whose history was written in unsafe places, that prediction system requires not just time – but the right experiences, accumulated slowly, to begin to revise its conclusions.*

The Vagal Brake and the Window of Social Engagement

Stephen Porges – whose polyvagal theory we will look at in more detail in Chapter 6 – offers a beautiful way of understanding what happens in the nervous system when we feel safe with another person. He describes a system he calls the social engagement system: a set of neural circuits connected to the vagus nerve that, when activated, signals safety to the whole body. It relaxes the muscles of the face. It opens the voice, giving it the warm, melodic quality that distinguishes friendly communication from threat. It orients the hearing toward the frequencies of human speech. It inhibits the defensive responses of the sympathetic system. In short, it puts the body in a state of open, curious, connected presence.

This system is activated by cues of safety – by a warm face, a calm voice, predictable and gentle behavior from another person. And for someone whose early life provided very few of these cues, the system may be chronically underactivated. The body stays in a mild defensive posture even in safe situations. The social engagement circuits do not fire as readily, because the nervous system never had enough consistent evidence of safety to learn to trust the activation.

This shows up in subtle ways. The person who cannot quite relax in social situations, even when there is no real threat. Who finds conversations effortful in ways they cannot explain. Whose body holds a kind of readiness even among friends. Who is told they seem distant or closed, when from the inside they feel anything but - they feel, in fact, quite desperate for the connection they cannot seem to fully achieve.

The good news - and there genuinely is good news, so stay with me here - is that the social engagement system is experience-dependent in both directions. It was shaped by the experience of early life. And it can be reshaped by the experience of later life. Slowly, incrementally, inconsistently, with a lot of two steps forward and one step back - but genuinely. The nervous system that learned to brace against human closeness can learn, through repeated experiences of safe closeness, to begin to unbrace.

This is not a quick process. It is measured in years, sometimes in decades. And it does not happen simply by deciding to trust people more. It happens by having experiences - real, embodied, repeated experiences - that accumulate new evidence. Evidence that contradicts the old model. Evidence that says: sometimes people stay. Sometimes closeness is safe. Sometimes the hand extended toward you is not about to become a fist.

The nervous system is a scientist. It changes its conclusions when it has enough new data. The question is just how long it takes to gather enough.

I want to pause here and say something to any reader who is recognizing themselves in this chapter - recognizing the anxious attachment, or the avoidant distance, or the disorganized chaos of wanting and fearing at the same time. Recognizing the internal working model. Recognizing the way trust does not come easily, the way closeness feels complicated, the way love - even when it is offered genuinely - somehow does not land where it should.

I know how heavy that recognition can be. Because it is one thing to have lived with these patterns without a name for them. And it is a strange and tender and sometimes grief-filled thing to finally see the pattern clearly - to understand where it came from, what it was doing, why it made perfect sense in the world that built it.

But I also want to say this, and I want to say it plainly before we move on: the pattern is not permanent. This is not just reassurance. This is neuroscience. We will come to this in much more detail later in the book, but the research on what is called earned secure attachment - the phenomenon of adults who began with insecure attachment and developed, through their own work and through safe relationships, the patterns of security - is one of the most hopeful bodies of research I know. It is real. It is documented. And it matters.

You did not write the first chapter of your story. But you are not finished writing.

What You Are Carrying - and That It Can Be Put Down

Attachment theory is sometimes misread as a story of damage. If your early attachment was insecure, if you never got the consistent, warm, responsive care that a child needs, then you are marked - broken in some fundamental way, doomed to repeat the patterns of your childhood in every relationship you ever have.

That reading is wrong. And it is important to say so clearly.

What attachment theory is actually saying is that early experience matters enormously, and that it creates patterns that persist - but that persist does not mean permanent. A pattern is a way of behaving that was learned. And what was learned can, in the right conditions, with the right support, over time and with enormous patience, be unlearned. Or more precisely: layered over with new learning, new experience, new data that the nervous system eventually - reluctantly, skeptically, but genuinely - accepts.

The internal working model is not carved in stone. It is written in a nervous system that, for all its conservatism, all its insistence on running the old program, is still alive. Still receiving information. Still, at some level, open to revision.

What you are carrying from your earliest experiences is real. The weight of it is real. The patterns it created in how you love, how you trust, how you experience closeness and distance and need - all of that is real and it deserves to be taken seriously, not minimized, not told to simply 'get over it.'

But it is also true that you are carrying it - which means it is not you. It is something you have. Something you learned. Something that can, over time, with the right kind of work and the right kind of relationships and the right kind of gentle, persistent attention to the patterns running quietly in the background - something that can slowly, slowly begin to change.

The map is wrong. But maps can be redrawn. That is what the rest of this book is about.

⊠ *Chapter 4: The Self That Survived*

4

The Self That Survived

Identity, Dissociation, and the Question of Who You Really Are

"The self is not a fixed thing. It is a story we are always revising - and sometimes, surviving."

Here is a question that sounds simple until you actually sit with it.

Who are you?

Not your name. Not your job or your nationality or the roles you play for other people. Not the version of yourself you present in different rooms. I mean the actual you - the one underneath all of that. The one that was there before the world started telling you who to be, and that is still there now, underneath everything that has been layered on top.

For most people, this question is mildly uncomfortable. A little philosophically dizzying, the way looking directly at the sun is dizzying. But they can answer it, more or less. They have a sense of themselves as a continuous person - someone who has been around since childhood, who carries memories from that childhood, who recognizes the thread between who they were at eight years old and who they are today, even if a lot has changed.

For people who grew up in traumatic environments, this question lands differently. Heavier. More complicated. Because trauma does something to the self that ordinary difficulty does not. It does not just challenge you. It fragments you. It creates gaps in the continuity, silences in the narrative, parts of the self that were put away somewhere - or never properly developed at all - because the environment required something other than wholeness. The environment required survival. And sometimes surviving means becoming many things, or becoming very small, or becoming whoever the room needs you to be. Sometimes it means not quite knowing, even now, who you are when there is no one watching. When the performance is not required. When you finally have a moment of stillness and the silence asks: okay. So. Who are you, really?

This chapter is about that question. It is about the self - what it is, how trauma shapes it, how parts of it get split off or buried or lost, and what it might mean to find it again. We are going to move between neuroscience and philosophy here, because this particular question requires both. The brain can tell us what happens to identity under threat. But philosophy has been asking who we are for thousands of years, and its questions are still the right ones.

4.1 - Dissociation: The Mind's Emergency Exit

Let me start with a word you may have encountered before, possibly in a clinical context, possibly misused in casual conversation until its actual meaning got blurred. Dissociation.

In everyday speech, people sometimes use it to mean spacing out - that mild drift of attention where you realize you have read the same sentence four times and absorbed nothing, or driven a familiar route without any memory of the journey. And that is indeed dissociation, at its mildest end. The spectrum is long.

At the other end of that spectrum is something much more intense - a fundamental disconnection between experience and consciousness, between what is happening to the body and what the mind can bear to register. A kind of internal exit. The mind, faced with something that is too much to process in the normal way, creates distance from it. Not by choosing to - this is not a decision - but automatically, the way a circuit breaker trips when the current gets too high. It is protective. It is adaptive. And in the context of trauma, it may have been the thing that kept a person intact when intact would otherwise have been impossible.

What Dissociation Actually Feels Like From the Inside

Dissociation is one of those experiences that is very common and almost never talked about clearly, partly because the clinical descriptions do not quite capture what it feels like to live inside it. So let me try to describe it in plain language.

> *Sometimes it feels like watching yourself from slightly outside your body - like being a spectator in your own life. You are doing things, saying things, existing in a room, but there is a faint sense of distance between you and all of it, as if there is a thin layer of glass separating you from your own experience. Things that should feel real feel slightly unreal. Emotions that should be present seem far away, muffled, like sounds heard through a closed door.*

This is called depersonalization - the sense of being detached from your own self - and it has a companion experience called derealization, where the world around you feels somehow off. Not quite solid. Not quite real. Like a film set that looks right but feels hollow. Both of these are the mind creating distance from an experience it cannot fully absorb.

There is also emotional dissociation - the ability to talk about something terrible that happened to you with a flatness, a calm, a detachment that surprises even you. Therapists sometimes see this and mistake it for healing, for acceptance, for having processed something. Often it is the opposite. It is the event being narrated from behind the glass. The words are present.

The felt reality is somewhere else.

And then there is the dissociation that most directly affects identity: the experience of not quite knowing who you are in a given moment. Of shifting, almost imperceptibly, between different ways of being - different tones, different emotional registers, different inner voices - in ways that can feel confusing and sometimes frightening. Not like being many people with entirely separate lives, as it is sometimes dramatized in popular culture, but like being a person with rooms that do not always connect. With parts that do not always speak to each other. With a self that sometimes feels coherent and sometimes feels like a collection of things that have not yet been organized into a whole.

> *Dissociation is not a malfunction. It is the mind's most elegant emergency response - a way of surviving what would otherwise be unsurvivable. The problem is that emergency responses, when they become habits, begin to cost more than they save.*

How Trauma Produces Dissociation - The Neuroscience

When something overwhelming happens - something that exceeds the brain's capacity to process it in real time - the normal memory consolidation process breaks down. Under ordinary circumstances, the hippocampus takes sensory and emotional information from an experience and weaves it into a coherent narrative memory: this happened, then this happened, then this happened, and here is how I felt, and now it is over and in the past. This narrative memory is what allows experience to be integrated - to become part of the continuous story of a life, past tense, contextual, finished.

Under conditions of extreme stress, this process fails. The hippocampus is flooded with cortisol and goes offline. The experience does not get woven into narrative. Instead, the raw sensory fragments - images, sounds, physical sensations, emotional states - get stored in the amygdala in their original unprocessed form. They do not become memories in the ordinary sense. They become more like live wires. Present tense. Accessible not as something that happened, but as something that is happening, whenever the nervous system encounters something that resembles the original experience.

Dissociation is partly the mind's response to this overload - a way of creating enough distance from the experience to prevent complete psychological collapse. And in childhood, when the brain is even more vulnerable and the child has even fewer resources for processing extreme experience, dissociation can become a habitual response. The default setting. The thing the mind does, automatically and efficiently, whenever the present moment becomes too much.

> *Research note: Studies using neuroimaging have found that people with trauma histories show reduced activity in the medial prefrontal cortex and increased activity in the amygdala during trauma recall - consistent with the pattern of poor integration between emotional and*

> *cognitive processing. Research by Ruth Lanius and colleagues has specifically shown that a subset of trauma survivors respond to threat cues with a dissociative pattern - reducing emotional reactivity through cortical suppression - rather than the hyperactivation seen in non-dissociative PTSD. This is the brain choosing numbness over flooding. Both are survival strategies.*

The challenge - and this is the challenge that follows dissociation out of childhood and into adult life - is that a response developed for genuine emergencies does not always stay confined to emergencies. It generalizes. It activates in situations that are stressful but not actually overwhelming. It becomes a habit of the mind. And a mind that habitually steps outside its own experience, that consistently creates distance between the self and what is being felt, gradually loses the ability to be fully present in its own life. To feel things fully. To be actually, completely, here.

4.2 - The Philosophy of Personal Identity and Trauma

Here is where we get to leave the laboratory for a moment and ask the questions that science, for all its power, cannot fully answer.

What makes you you? What makes the person reading these words right now the same person who was a child in a house somewhere, learning the lessons that house was teaching? Is there a continuous self that persisted through all of it - the frightening parts, the lonely parts, the parts you would rather not remember? Or is the self something more fragmented, more constructed, more like a story being told than a fixed thing being carried?

Philosophers have been arguing about personal identity for a very long time. John Locke, in the seventeenth century, proposed that personal identity is constituted by memory - you are the same person across time because you can remember being that person. What connects the adult to the child is the chain of memories linking them. This is a tidy theory, and it works reasonably well for people with uninterrupted access to their memories.

But trauma complicates it immediately. What about the memories you cannot access? What about the years that are blurry, or the specific events that are simply gone - dissociated, buried, stored in a form the conscious mind cannot retrieve? If identity is memory, and memory is disrupted or absent, what happens to the self in those gaps? Is there a self there at all? Or is there something like a self - a presence that persisted, that kept going, that managed somchow to continue existing through the parts of experience that the conscious mind could not hold?

David Hume and the Bundle Theory: No Self, Just Stories

The eighteenth-century Scottish philosopher David Hume sat down to try to find his self - to look inward and locate the thing that was doing the looking - and reported something startling. He could not find it. What he found, instead, was a stream of perceptions, thoughts, feelings, images - one after another, constantly flowing, constantly changing. But no fixed observer. No stable core. Just the stream.

Hume concluded that the self is not a thing. It is a bundle of experiences - a narrative we construct to give the impression of continuity, of being someone who persists through time. There is no ghost in the machine. There is just the machine, and the stories it tells about itself.

This might sound bleak. But for people with trauma histories, I find Hume's theory oddly liberating. Because if the self is a narrative rather than a fixed thing - a story rather than a stone - then the story is not finished. It was never fixed. The version that was written in childhood, the character that the traumatic environment shaped, is a version. Not the version. Not the final draft. A draft that was written under particular conditions, with particular materials, by a particular child doing their best in a difficult situation. And it can be revised.

Derek Parfit and the Ship of Theseus: What Survives When Everything Changes

Derek Parfit was a twentieth-century philosopher who spent much of his career thinking about personal identity in ways that were simultaneously deeply technical and profoundly humane. One of his central observations was that we are not the same person across time in any strict sense. The cells in your body replace themselves. Your beliefs, values, memories, personality - all of it changes, slowly or sometimes dramatically, across a life. The child you were and the adult you are share a name and a history, but very little else.

And Parfit thought this was, in the end, good news. Because if there is no fixed self that persists unchanged through time, then the self is not a prison. You are not locked into being the person you were. The person who was shaped by a traumatic childhood is connected to you - shares your history, your body, your name - but is not exactly you. And the person you will be in ten years is connected to who you are now, but will not be exactly you either. The self is a river, not a stone. Always moving, always becoming something slightly different, never entirely the same from one moment to the next.

> *If who you are is something that keeps changing - and it is, always, for everyone - then the person the trauma made you is not the last word. It is a chapter. A long one, sometimes. A hard one, often. But a chapter, not the whole book.*

The Neuroscience of Self: The Default Mode Network

The brain has a specific system for constructing and maintaining the sense of self. It is called the default mode network - a constellation of brain regions that become particularly active when we are not focused on an external task. When we are daydreaming, reflecting, remembering, imagining the future, thinking about other people, or thinking about ourselves. It is the brain's introspective system. The neural home of the self-as-story.

In people with trauma histories, the default mode network

functions differently. It is often less coherent - the regions that should be communicating with each other do not do so as fluidly. The capacity for self-reflection, for a stable and continuous inner narrative, is disrupted. Some people describe this as a difficulty knowing what they feel, or what they want, or what they actually think as opposed to what they have learned they are supposed to think. A kind of inner static. A haziness where the self should be clear.

This is not a sign that there is no self. It is a sign that the neural infrastructure for self-awareness and self-continuity was built under difficult conditions and runs with a particular kind of noise. The self is there. It is just harder to hear over the static. And learning to hear it - learning to turn the static down - is one of the central projects of recovery.

4.3 - The Hidden Self: Concealment as Identity

There is a specific form of self-fragmentation that does not come only from what happened to you - from the abuse or the neglect or the chaos of the home. It also comes from what you had to hide. From the parts of yourself that were not safe to show. From the learning, early and thorough, that certain things about you - your feelings, your needs, your fears, your true reactions to things - were not welcome. Were dangerous. Would cost you something you could not afford to pay.

And for some people, this goes even deeper. Because there is a dimension of identity that goes beyond behavior and feeling - a dimension of who you fundamentally are - that, in some environments and some families and some cultures, must be hidden completely. Not just managed. Erased from the visible surface of a life.

I am talking about the experience of growing up with an identity that the world around you has told you is wrong. Shameful. Something to be fixed or denied or prayed away. The experience of being gay, or bisexual, or trans, or in any other way different from what the people around you assumed you were, in a world that was not safe for that truth.

The closet is many things. It is a social structure, a survival strategy, a form of daily performance that requires enormous energy and leaves enormous residue. But it is also, I want to argue, a specific kind of wound to the self. Because the self that is hidden - that is locked away, that is never allowed to be seen - does not simply wait patiently in the dark until the door is opened. It develops in the dark. It grows strange and complicated in the dark. And the person who has spent years performing a self they are not, for an audience that would not be safe with the truth, often arrives at adulthood not knowing quite where the performance ends and the person begins.

The Cost of Sustained Concealment

Psychologist James Pennebaker spent years studying what happens to people when they keep significant secrets - when there is something important and emotionally loaded that they cannot tell anyone. What he found was not surprising in broad terms but striking in its specificity. The active inhibition of thoughts, feelings, and behaviors - the ongoing work of not saying the thing, not showing the feeling, not being who you are - is physiologically expensive. It activates the sympathetic nervous system. It elevates cortisol. It suppresses immune function. It is, quite literally, stressful in the biological sense.

Over years and decades, sustained concealment of a core identity accumulates these costs. The mental load of managing two selves - the visible one and the real one - is not trivial. It requires constant monitoring: of what you say and how you say it, of which pronouns you use and which stories you tell and which feelings you allow yourself to show and which you immediately suppress. It is like running a second program in the background of every interaction, every relationship, every ordinary moment of being in the world with other people.

And the self that is doing all this managing - the one that has been in performance mode since before it could properly define what it was performing against - often loses track of itself. Not dramatically. Not all at once. But gradually, in the way that a voice loses its accent when it speaks a different language long enough. The authentic self does not disappear. But it becomes quieter. Less certain of itself. Less practiced at being real, because being real has never been safe enough to practice.

> *There is something particular about realizing, as an adult, that you do not know what you actually like - what you actually enjoy, what you actually want - separate from what you learned to perform wanting. That the preferences, the personality, the way of moving through the world that you have presented to everyone is a version so carefully managed that you are not entirely sure what is underneath it. Not because there is nothing*

there. But because you have not had much practice at looking.

> *The hidden self is not a false self. It is the real self that never had a safe place to be real. It is still there. It has always been there. It just needs, finally, to be allowed to exist without the constant threat of consequence.*

Coming Out as Coming Home - To Yourself

There is a reason people who come out - as gay, as their true gender, as carrying a history they have never spoken aloud, as anything they have had to hide - so often describe the experience as a homecoming. Not just a social event. Not just a change in how others see them. A return to something. A meeting with a self that has been waiting.

But it is rarely that simple, of course. Because the self that comes out of hiding has been in hiding, and hiding changes things. The person who spent years being someone else has to learn, in some ways, to be themselves. To tolerate being seen. To unlearn the reflexive monitoring, the constant management of presentation. To sit with the discomfort of being known and resist the impulse to immediately hide again.

And for those whose concealment was layered on top of other wounds - who were hiding their identity and hiding their trauma and hiding their pain, all at once, with no one to help carry any of it - the unfolding is slower and more complicated and requires more gentleness than anyone quite tells you it will.

We will return to this - to the specific experience of carrying both trauma and a hidden identity, and what that compounding does to a person - in Chapter 10, when we talk about love and relationships. For now, I want to simply name it. To say: the cost of hiding who you are is real. It shows up in the nervous system, in the immune system, in the fragmented sense of self, in the exhaustion that does not have an obvious source. And the work of coming out of hiding - whatever form that hiding took - is not just social or political. It is biological. It is psychological. It is, in the deepest sense, a healing.

4.4 - Authenticity After Trauma: Is It Possible?

The existentialists - Sartre, Heidegger, Camus, that particular group of serious Europeans who spent the mid-twentieth century being magnificently, productively gloomy - had a concept they called authenticity. And it is a concept worth spending time with, because it is one of the most useful ideas philosophy has produced, especially for people trying to understand who they are after trauma.

For Heidegger, authenticity meant something specific: existing in full ownership of your own life. Not falling into what he called das Man - the anonymous 'they,' the crowd, the pressure to be what people expect, to want what people want, to live as though your life belongs to some general public rather than to yourself. Authentic existence meant facing your own finitude, your own particular situation, your own choices - and making them deliberately, as yourself, rather than drifting along in the comfortable unreality of performing what is expected.

This is a high bar. And for most people it is an aspiration rather than a steady state. But for someone who grew up in an environment that actively punished authenticity - that required performance of safety, of happiness, of a self that the environment could tolerate - the bar is higher still. Because the drift toward das Man was not a philosophical laziness. It was survival. The authentic self was a liability. The performed self was the thing that kept you safe.

The Difference Between Authenticity and Certainty

Here is something I want to name carefully, because I think it matters for people who are working on this.

Authenticity does not require certainty about who you are. This is a mistake people make - thinking that being authentic means having a clear, settled, fully resolved sense of self that you then present to the world with confidence. As if you have to figure yourself out completely before you are allowed to exist as yourself.

That is not what authenticity means. Authenticity is not a destination. It is a practice. It is the practice of being honest about where you are - including being honest about the confusion, the uncertainty, the parts of yourself you have not yet understood or integrated. It is possible to be completely authentic while also being completely lost. In fact, for many people who grew up in traumatic environments, admitting that you are lost - saying it out loud, without performing a certainty you do not feel - is itself the most authentic thing they have done in years.

> *You do not need to know who you are before you can start being it. You just need to stop pretending to be something you are not. The self that remains, uncertain and incomplete, is still more real than the performance.*

The Constructed Self: A Feature, Not a Bug

Let me offer a reframe that I find genuinely useful, and that both the neuroscience and the philosophy support.

The self is constructed. Always. By everyone. Not just by trauma survivors. Every human self is built from experience, from the particular environment it grew up in, from the relationships it was shaped by, from the culture and family and historical moment it happened to arrive in. Nobody's self arrives fully formed, untouched by circumstance. The self is always, to some degree, made rather than found.

What trauma does is make this construction visible in ways that are usually invisible. The person who grew up in safety can feel like their self is just naturally who they are - spontaneous, continuous, unmediated. The person who grew up in chaos can see clearly that their self was built from particular materials under particular pressures, because the building process was harder and the materials were more difficult. But the person in safety is also constructed. Their self also emerged from conditions. They just happened to be better conditions.

What this means, practically, is this: if the self is constructed, it can be reconstructed. Not from scratch - you are not starting over, and the person you have been is real and valuable and part of what you are working with. But the construction is not finished. It was never finished. And the person who can see, clearly and honestly, that their self was built from particular materials under particular conditions - that person is in a better position to make deliberate choices about what gets added next than the person who believes their self is simply given, fixed, and out of their hands.

This is one of the quiet gifts that trauma, looked at honestly and from the right angle, can offer. Not a gift that compensates for what it cost - nothing does that. But a gift nonetheless: the clarity that the self is yours to work with. That it was not handed to you complete and immutable. That it is alive, and changing, and something you participate in making.

✦✦✦

I want to close this chapter with something a little more personal than what I usually allow myself, because I think it belongs here.

The question of who you are, when everything that shaped you was difficult - when the house was dangerous and the love was absent or conditional and the parts of you that were most truly yourself had to be hidden - that question is not an abstract philosophical puzzle. It is lived. It is felt in the morning, when you wake up and have a moment before the day starts and you catch, just for a second, a glimpse of something underneath all the constructions. It is felt in the middle of conversations, when something true almost surfaces and then recedes because the habit of concealment is faster than the impulse to be real.

That glimpse is real. The thing that almost surfaced is real. The you that exists underneath the performances and the adaptations and the ways you learned to be in order to survive - that person is real.

They did not disappear during the difficult years. They were there. They were the one watching, even when they could not act. They were the one who kept asking questions - kept reading, kept thinking, kept being curious about the world despite everything - because curiosity was one of the things the environment could not fully take. They were the one who made it this far.

And they are the one reading these words right now, wondering - maybe - whether it is possible to come home to themselves. Whether the distance between who they had to be and who they actually are can be closed. Whether the self that survived the house is something they can finally, carefully, begin to inhabit.

The answer, in my experience and in the science, is yes. Not quickly. Not without difficulty. Not in a straight line. But yes.

The Self Is Not a Ruin. It Is a Work in Progress.

We have covered a lot of ground in this chapter. Dissociation - what it is, why it happens, how it becomes a habit that outlives its usefulness. The philosophy of personal identity - Locke, Hume, Parfit - and what it means that the self is a story rather than a fixed thing. The hidden self - the cost of sustained concealment, and the particular wound of having to hide a fundamental truth about who you are. And authenticity - what it actually means, how it is a practice rather than a destination, and how the visible construction of the traumatized self is not a disadvantage but a clarity that most people are never forced to develop.

The thread running through all of it is this: you are not who trauma made you. Or rather - you are partly who trauma made you, because that is inescapable and honest. But you are also the one who survived it. The one who is still here, still asking, still capable of reflection and growth and the hard, patient work of becoming more yourself. The self that was fragmented can be gathered. The self that was hidden can be revealed. The self that was constructed from difficult materials can be given better ones.

None of this is fast. None of it is linear. None of it happens just because you understand it intellectually, though understanding is always a beginning. It happens through experience, through relationship, through the slow accumulation of moments in which you are more yourself than you were the moment before.

That is the work. And it is worth doing. Not because the past deserved to happen, but because the future does not have to look like it.

⊠ *Chapter 5: The Darkness That Moves In*

II

The Weight

Depression, somatic experience, social masking, and economic adversity as lived dimensions of the long aftermath of early wounds.

5

The Darkness That Moves In

Depression, Major Depressive Disorder, and the Biology of Despair

"Depression is not sadness. Sadness still believes the world is worth crying about."

Let me tell you what depression is not, before I tell you what it is.

Depression is not a bad day. It is not the grief you feel when something terrible happens - when you lose someone you love, or a relationship ends, or a dream you were carrying turns out to be impossible. Those things hurt. They hurt terribly. But they are not depression. They are normal human responses to loss, and they have a shape and a trajectory and, eventually, a softening. Time, in those cases, genuinely helps. The acute pain dulls. Life eventually reasserts itself. You find, somehow, a way to continue.

Depression is different. Depression is when the pain has no obvious source, or when the source is long past but the pain remains. It is when you wake up and the world is still there - the sun is still coming up, people are still going about their lives - and you cannot feel any of it. Not sadness, exactly. Numbness. Flatness. A color drained out of everything. The things that used to matter do not matter. The activities that used to bring pleasure bring nothing. The future, which used to stretch out with possibility, now just stretches - blank, heavy, indistinguishable from the present.

And here is the thing that nobody quite tells you about major depressive disorder, the clinical name for the experience I am describing: it is not just psychological. It is not just in your head, in the dismissive sense people sometimes use that phrase. It is in your brain. It is in your body. It is in the neurochemistry, the immune system, the way your cells metabolize energy. It is biological in ways that are measurable, specific, and profoundly disruptive to almost every system that keeps a human being functioning.

This chapter is about that darkness. What it is, where it comes from, why it follows trauma the way a shadow follows a body. We are going to be honest about how hard it is, because pretending otherwise would be a disservice to anyone living inside it. But we are also going to be precise about the science - because understanding the mechanism is one of the few things that helps when the darkness is telling you that nothing helps.

5.1 - What Depression Actually Is: Beyond the Serotonin Myth

For decades, if you asked a doctor what causes depression, you would get a simple answer: a chemical imbalance. Specifically, not enough serotonin in the brain. The pharmaceutical companies built entire marketing campaigns around this idea. Prozac, Zoloft, Lexapro - all of them selective serotonin reuptake inhibitors, or SSRIs - were presented as a way to fix the imbalance. Like diabetes, which is an insulin problem, depression was a serotonin problem. Take the pill, restore the balance, feel better.

The only issue with this explanation is that it was never quite true. Or more precisely: it was a simplification that went so far past the actual complexity of the science that it became misleading.

Here is what we actually know. SSRIs do help some people - genuinely, measurably, not through placebo alone. For about thirty to forty percent of people with major depression, SSRIs produce significant relief. But the mechanism by which they help is far more complicated than simply restoring a serotonin deficit. In fact, the serotonin levels in the brain increase within hours of taking an SSRI, but the therapeutic effects - when they occur - take weeks. If depression were simply low serotonin, the timeline would not make sense.

What seems to be happening, based on decades of more sophisticated research, is that serotonin is not the endpoint. It is a catalyst. SSRIs increase serotonin availability, yes. But what that increase serotonin does - when it works - is trigger a cascade of downstream effects: increased brain-derived neurotrophic factor (BDNF), which supports neuroplasticity; reduced inflammation in the brain; changes in the default mode network and the connectivity between brain regions; and, over time, the actual regrowth of neural connections in areas like the hippocampus that had atrophied under chronic stress.

Depression, in other words, is not a deficit of one chemical. It is a systemic dysregulation of multiple interacting systems - neurochemical, neurostructural, inflammatory, metabolic - that together produce the experience of a brain and body that have stopped functioning the way they are supposed to.

> *Depression is not something you have. It is something your whole system is doing - a state the body has entered, for reasons that are usually multiple and compounding, and that requires more than a single chemical adjustment to exit.*

The Inflammation Hypothesis: When the Immune System Attacks the Mind

One of the most important shifts in depression research over the last two decades has been the recognition that inflammation - the immune system's response to injury or infection - plays a central role in a significant subset of depressive disorders.

Here is how it works. When the body is under chronic stress - and childhood trauma counts as chronic stress, even if it is not happening anymore, because the body's stress-response system stays activated long after the danger has passed - the immune system goes into a state of low-grade, persistent activation. Pro-inflammatory cytokines like interleukin-6 and tumor necrosis factor-alpha circulate at higher-than-normal levels. These cytokines do not stay in the periphery. They cross the blood-brain barrier. And once they are in the brain, they interfere with the very systems that regulate mood, motivation, and energy.

Specifically, inflammation disrupts the production and metabolism of serotonin, dopamine, and norepinephrine - the neurotransmitters most implicated in mood regulation. It reduces neuroplasticity. It activates the HPA axis, which we talked about in Chapter 2, keeping the stress system in a state of chronic alarm. And it produces what researchers call sickness behavior: fatigue, social withdrawal, loss of appetite, difficulty concentrating, anhedonia - the inability to feel pleasure. All of which, you will notice, are also core symptoms of major depression.

The body, in other words, is treating depression as if it were an infection. The immune system is responding to a threat - and for people with trauma histories, the threat was real, and the response made sense at the time. The problem is that the immune system, like the amygdala, does not always know when the war is over. It keeps fighting. And the collateral damage is the mind.

Research note: A 2020 meta-analysis by Kohler and colleagues found that approximately one-third of people with major depression show elevated markers of systemic inflammation, and that this subset tends to respond poorly to traditional SSRIs but better to treatments that target inflammation directly, such as anti-inflammatory drugs or lifestyle interventions like exercise. The inflammation is not incidental. For some people, it is the mechanism.

Neuroplasticity and the Brain That Stopped Growing

Another dimension of what depression does - and this is one of the findings that has most changed how neuroscientists think about the disorder - is that it suppresses neuroplasticity. The brain's capacity to form new connections, to adapt, to learn, to change in response to experience - all of this is dampened in major depression.

Brain imaging studies consistently show reduced volume in the hippocampus of people with chronic depression. Not just reduced activity. Reduced size. Fewer neurons. Less connectivity. And the longer the depression persists, the more pronounced the atrophy. This is not permanent brain damage in the sense of being irreversible - we will come back to that - but it is structural change. The brain, under the conditions of chronic depression, quite literally shrinks in certain areas.

And this has functional consequences. The hippocampus is involved in memory, yes, but also in regulation of the HPA axis - the stress system. A damaged hippocampus cannot effectively tell the stress system to stand down. Which means the stress continues. Which means more cortisol. Which means more hippocampal damage. Which means less effective stress regulation. The loop feeds itself.

This is why depression can feel like a trap. Because in some very real neurological sense, it is one. The state of the brain under depression makes it harder for the brain to exit that state. The very systems that would be needed to recover are the systems that depression has impaired.

5.2 - Trauma and Depression: The Biological Pipeline

Depression and trauma are not the same thing. You can have one without the other. But the overlap between them is enormous, consistent, and backed by some of the clearest data in all of psychiatry.

The ACE Study, which we discussed in Chapter 2, found that adults with high ACE scores - meaning multiple categories of childhood adversity - were between four and twelve times more likely to develop depression than those with no childhood adversity. Four to twelve times. That is not a small effect. That is one of the strongest predictive relationships in public health research.

And it is not just correlation. We can trace the mechanism - the biological pathway that connects childhood trauma to adult depression - with increasing precision.

The HPA Axis: The Stress System That Never Resets

We have talked about the HPA axis - the hypothalamic-pituitary-adrenal axis - in previous chapters, but I want to return to it here because it is central to understanding how trauma becomes depression.

In a person who grew up in a safe and stable environment, the HPA axis responds to acute stressors in a predictable way: threat is detected, cortisol is released, the body mobilizes, the threat passes, cortisol levels drop, the system returns to baseline. Alarm, response, resolution. The cycle completes.

In a person who grew up in chronic threat - in domestic violence, in neglect, in the persistent unpredictability of a chaotic home - the HPA axis never gets to complete that cycle. The alarm goes off constantly. Cortisol stays elevated. And over time, the system does something that is both adaptive and damaging: it recalibrates.

Sometimes the recalibration looks like hyperactivation - the system becomes even more reactive, flooding the body with cortisol in response to minor stressors. Sometimes it looks like hypoactivation - the system becomes blunted, producing less cortisol than it should, as if it has exhausted itself from overuse. Both patterns - hyperactivation and hypoactivation - are associated with depression. Both represent a stress system that is no longer functioning in a way that supports wellbeing.

And here is the connection to depression: cortisol, at chronically elevated levels, is toxic to the very brain regions that regulate mood. The hippocampus, as we have discussed. The prefrontal cortex, which manages executive function and emotional regulation. Even the reward circuits in the brain - the systems that allow you to feel pleasure, to anticipate good things, to want anything - are disrupted by prolonged cortisol exposure.

Trauma rewires the stress system. The rewired stress system produces chronic cortisol dysregulation. The cortisol dysregulation damages the brain structures that regulate mood and motivation. And the result, in far too many cases, is depression. Not as a psychological reaction to the trauma - though that is also real - but as a biological consequence of it. The pipeline is direct. The mechanism is clear.

> *Childhood trauma does not just make you sad about what happened. It changes the biology of how your brain handles stress, pleasure, and hope - and those changes can persist long after the danger is gone.*

Learned Helplessness and the Brain That Stopped Trying

There is a concept from psychology - originally from animal research, but replicated in humans in ways that are both illuminating and deeply sad - called learned helplessness. And it is one of the most powerful models we have for understanding how chronic adversity produces depression.

In the 1960s, psychologist Martin Seligman conducted a series of experiments with dogs. The dogs were placed in a situation where they received mild electric shocks. Some of the dogs could escape the shocks by pressing a lever. Others could not - the lever did nothing, and the shocks came regardless of what the dog did. After a period of this inescapable stress, the dogs were moved to a new situation where escape was possible. But the dogs that had previously experienced inescapable stress did not even try to escape. They just lay down and endured the shocks, even though a simple action would have stopped them. They had learned that their actions did not matter. They had learned helplessness.

The neurological changes that accompanied this behavioral change were striking. The dogs that developed learned helplessness showed reduced levels of serotonin and norepinephrine in the brain. They showed changes in the prefrontal cortex and the hippocampus. They showed, in other words, the biological signature of depression.

Now translate this to a child. A child in a home where the adults are unpredictable. Where being good does not guarantee safety. Where trying to please, trying to be invisible, trying to manage the situation - none of it reliably works. The child learns, at a visceral level, that their actions do not determine outcomes. That the world is not responsive to their efforts. That trying is futile.

This is not a conscious belief, necessarily. It is deeper than belief. It is a learned prediction about how the world works, encoded in the same systems that encode all predictions: the dopamine pathways that signal reward and motivation, the prefrontal cortex that plans and initiates action, the very sense of agency that allows a person to feel like a person who can do things rather than a person to whom things are done.

And when that sense of agency is damaged early - when the child learns that effort does not lead to relief, that there is no action they can take to make things better - that learning does not simply disappear when the child becomes an adult. It stays. It becomes the baseline expectation. It becomes the quiet voice that says, under every difficulty: what is the point of trying? It will not work anyway. It never does.

That voice is not laziness. It is not weakness. It is learned helplessness. And it is one of the most common and most invisible symptoms of depression in trauma survivors.

5.3 - The Phenomenology of Major Depression

I want to shift registers here for a moment. We have been talking about mechanisms - cortisol, inflammation, neuroplasticity, the HPA axis. All of that is real and important. But depression is not lived as a mechanism. It is lived as an experience. And the experience of major depression is something that the clinical language often fails to capture.

Philosopher Matthew Ratcliffe has written extensively about what he calls the phenomenology of depression - the study of what it actually feels like, from the inside, to exist in a depressed state. And one of his central observations is that depression is not primarily about being sad. It is about a fundamental alteration in how possibility itself feels.

The Collapse of the Future

In ordinary experience, the future exists as a space of potential. Things could happen. You could do things. The world ahead of you contains possibilities that are not yet determined, and you - through your actions, your choices, your efforts - participate in which of those possibilities becomes real. This basic sense of futurity, of openness, of time stretching forward with some degree of malleability, is so fundamental to normal consciousness that most people never notice it. It is just the way time feels.

In depression, that sense collapses. The future does not feel open. It feels closed, predetermined, indistinguishable from the present. Nothing you do will change anything, because nothing can change. The heaviness you feel now is the heaviness you will feel tomorrow, and next week, and next year. The future is not a space of possibility. It is just more of this. The same gray weight, extending forward without variation, without exit.

Ratcliffe calls this a loss of existential hope - not hope for a specific outcome, but hope as the basic structure of temporal experience. The felt sense that the future could be different from the present. That change is possible. That time moves, and brings with it the possibility of something new. Depression does not just make you pessimistic about the future. It makes the future unreal. Unreachable. A concept rather than a lived horizon.

> *Depression does not just make you sad. It changes the shape of time – flattening the future into an extension of a present that feels like it will never end.*

Anhedonia: When Nothing Feels Like Anything

One of the core diagnostic criteria for major depressive disorder is something called anhedonia: the inability to experience pleasure. But that clinical term does not quite capture what it feels like.

It is not that things you used to enjoy are now less enjoyable. It is that the entire capacity to feel enjoyment seems to have been switched off. You can still do things – go through the motions of activities that used to bring pleasure – but there is no affective response. No lightness. No lift. You are present in the experience but not moved by it. It is like watching a movie with the sound off, or eating food when you have a cold and cannot taste anything. The thing is happening. You are just not in it.

This is neurologically specific. The brain's reward system – particularly the ventral striatum and the dopamine pathways that signal anticipation and pleasure – shows reduced activity in depression. The anticipation of reward, which in a healthy brain produces a surge of dopamine that feels like wanting, does not fire. The experience of reward, which should produce a sense of satisfaction, registers as nothing. The system is intact, structurally. It is just not responding.

And the absence of pleasure is not a neutral state. It is its own kind of suffering. Because a life without pleasure is not simply boring or dull. It is exhausting. Every activity requires effort - the effort of making yourself do the thing - without any of the reward that would make the effort feel worthwhile. The entire motivational economy of being a person collapses. Why would you do anything, if doing it feels like nothing?

> *You sit with friends who are laughing, and you understand intellectually that something funny was said. You can see them enjoying themselves. But you are behind glass. The laughter does not reach you. Or you finish a project - something that used to bring satisfaction, pride, a sense of accomplishment - and you feel nothing. Just tired. Just the next thing to do. The reward system that would have made it worth doing is offline, and you are left with the bare effort of existing, uncompensated by any felt sense that the existence is worth the work.*

The Exhaustion That Sleep Does Not Fix

There is a particular kind of tiredness that comes with depression that people who have not experienced it often misunderstand. It is not the tiredness of having worked hard, or of not getting enough sleep, though those can be part of it. It is a fatigue that is constitutional - in your bones, in your cells, in the basic effort of being awake and conscious and navigating the ordinary demands of a day.

You sleep for ten hours and wake up exhausted. You do nothing all day and feel as drained as if you had run a marathon. The effort of answering an email feels monumental. The prospect of a social interaction - even with people you love - feels like being asked to climb a mountain.

This is not laziness. This is the metabolic consequence of a brain and body that are working enormously hard at the cellular level to manage a state of chronic dysregulation. Inflammation, cortisol, disrupted sleep architecture, reduced mitochondrial function - all of these are present in depression, and all of them produce fatigue. Real, physical, measurable fatigue. The kind that does not respond to rest, because the problem is not that you have expended energy. The problem is that your system is not producing energy efficiently in the first place.

5.4 - Ten Years in the Dark: Living With Chronic Depression

Most of what gets written about depression - in clinical literature, in self-help books, in the media - assumes that depression is episodic. You have an episode. It is awful. You get treatment. You recover. Maybe it comes back. Maybe it does not. But the model is one of distinct episodes separated by periods of wellness.

For many people, that is not how it works. For many people,

depression is not an episode. It is a climate. A persistent, low-grade - or sometimes high-grade - state that lasts not for weeks or months but for years. Sometimes for decades. This is what clinicians call chronic depression, or persistent depressive disorder, or dysthymia when it is less severe but still unrelenting.

And living with chronic depression is a different thing entirely from living through a depressive episode. Because when depression is your baseline, you do not have the memory of wellness to hold onto. You do not wake up one day and realize you feel better, because you have no clear sense of what better would feel like. The depression is not an intrusion into your life. It is your life. It is the medium through which you experience everything.

The Erosion of Self

One of the things chronic depression does that acute depression often does not is slowly erode your sense of who you are outside of it.

In the beginning - the first year, maybe two - there is still a sense that this is something happening to you. A state you are in, but not identical with. You are a person who is depressed, which means there is still a you underneath the depression, waiting to re-emerge once the depression lifts.

But at some point, if the depression does not lift - if it just continues, year after year, becoming the constant background hum of your existence - the distinction starts to blur. Are you a person who is depressed, or are you just this? Is there a self underneath the depression, or is the depression all there is? The question starts to feel unanswerable, because you cannot remember clearly enough what you were like before to know if there is a difference.

This is one of the quietest and most devastating aspects of long-term depression: the way it absorbs the self. Not dramatically. Not all at once. But slowly, over years, until you are no longer sure where you end and the illness begins.

The Practical Costs: Work, Relationships, Time

Chronic depression has costs that are mundane, practical, and enormous.

Careers that stall or never start, because the energy required to pursue them is not available. Relationships that erode, because you do not have the capacity to show up for other people in the ways they need, and because being around someone who is perpetually low-energy and emotionally flat is, for most people, eventually exhausting. Time that disappears - not spent on anything in particular, just lost to the effort of getting through the day.

And these costs compound. The longer depression persists, the more the gap grows between where you are and where you feel like you should be. Your peers are advancing in careers, forming families, building lives, and you are still just trying to get through the week without falling apart. The gap itself becomes another source of despair. Not just 'I feel terrible now,' but 'I have lost years to this, and I will never get them back.'

There is a particular loneliness to chronic depression that acute depression does not quite have. Because most people can relate to being sad, or going through a hard time, or struggling for a few months. But most people cannot relate to a decade of barely holding on. To being functional enough that nobody quite recognizes how much effort it takes you to do ordinary things, but not functional enough to build the kind of life you imagined. To existing in that gray zone where you are not quite sick enough to stop, but not well enough to thrive.

> *Chronic depression is not dramatic. It is the slow accumulation of days that feel the same, that cost more than they give, that leave you wondering - quietly, persistently, without much hope of an answer - if this is all there is.*

Why People Stay Alive - And Why That Matters

I want to talk about something that is hard to talk about, but that belongs in this chapter because it is real and common and deserves to be addressed honestly.

When you have been depressed for a very long time - when you have spent years, or a decade, in the dark - the question of whether to continue starts to present itself. Not necessarily in a dramatic, acute, crisis-driven way. But quietly. Persistently.

As a rational question about whether a life that feels like this is worth the effort it requires.

And I want to say something about that question that I think the mental health field sometimes gets wrong. The question is not irrational. For someone living in severe, unrelenting, treatment-resistant depression, the question of whether to continue is not a symptom to be dismissed or a cognitive distortion to be corrected. It is a serious existential question that deserves a serious answer.

The answer that I have found most useful - both personally and in the literature - is not 'life is always worth living' or 'suicide is never the answer' or any of the other platitudes that get offered. The answer is this: the state you are in right now is not the only state you will ever be in. Even if you have been in it for a very long time. Even if it feels permanent. The brain is capable of change in ways that are not always visible from inside the depressed state. The future is not reliably knowable. And as long as you are alive, there is some nonzero probability that the state will shift.

That is not false hope. It is uncertainty. And uncertainty, when you are in the dark, is enough. It is the thing that keeps people going - not the belief that things will definitely get better, but the acknowledgment that they might. That the future is not as closed as depression makes it feel. That possibility, in some form, still exists.

If you are reading this and recognizing yourself - if you have been in the dark for a long time like me, I spent 10 years in this, and are tired and are wondering whether you can keep doing this - I want to say this directly. You can. Not because I believe in some inevitable arc toward wellness, but because the fact that you are still here, still reading, still asking the questions, means that some part of you is still oriented toward the future. Even if it is a very small part. Even if it is barely holding on. That part is real. And it deserves to be listened to.

✦✦✦

I am going to close this section, and this chapter, with something that is important to say and that the research supports but that people often do not hear clearly enough.

Depression - even chronic, severe, decade-long depression - is not a life sentence. Not in the legal sense, and not in the neurological sense. The brain that is depressed is not a broken brain. It is a brain in a particular state, shaped by particular biology, often in response to particular history. And states can change. Not easily. Not quickly. Not without help and work and, often, a lot of trial and error. But genuinely.

We will talk in Part Three of this book about what recovery actually looks like, what the science supports, and what people who have made it through to the other side have learned. For now, I just want to hold the space for the possibility. The fact that you have been in the dark for a long time does not mean you will be in the dark forever. That is not a guarantee. But it is a real possibility. And possibility is sometimes all you need to make it to the next day.

The Weight of What Was Carried - And That It Can Be Set Down

This has been, I know, a difficult chapter. There is no way to talk honestly about depression without naming how heavy it is, how long it can last, how much it costs. And if you are reading this from the inside of it, I know how strange it can feel to have your experience described - both the relief of recognition and the weight of seeing it laid out in such stark terms.

What I hope you take from this chapter is not a sense of doom, but a sense of clarity. Depression is not a character flaw. It is not weakness. It is not evidence that you are not trying hard enough or thinking positively enough or doing the right things. It is a state that the brain and body enter, often for very good biological reasons, in response to experiences that genuinely warranted a strong stress response.

And here is the thing the science keeps showing: the brain that entered that state can exit it. Not through willpower alone. Not through simply deciding to feel better. But through the slow accumulation of the right kinds of experiences, the right kinds of interventions, the right kinds of relationships and environments and, sometimes, medications. The biology that was shaped one way can be shaped another way. The neuroplasticity that depression suppresses can, under the right conditions, be restored.

The darkness you are carrying is real. The weight of it is real. And you did not choose to carry it. But you are carrying it. Which means you are strong in ways that most people will never have to be. And that strength - the sheer, exhausting, invisible strength of continuing to exist through something this heavy - is worth naming.

The next chapters will move through the body, through the social world, through the economics of surviving. And then, in Part Three, we will turn toward what healing looks like when healing is possible. For now, if you are in it, know this: you are not alone in it. And the fact that you have made it this far means something.

⊠ *Chapter 6: The Body Keeps the Score*

6

The Body Keeps the Score

Somatic Experience, Physical Health, and the Flesh That Carries the Past

"Long after the mind tries to move on, the body is still standing in that room."

I spent eight years standing in front of classrooms teaching biology. Cellular respiration, photosynthesis, the Krebs cycle, evolution, genetics - the material I knew so well that I could have taught it in my sleep. And some days, it felt like I was.

I would walk into the lecture hall, smile at the students, write the day's topic on the board in handwriting that was supposed to look confident, and then - in the middle of explaining something I had explained a hundred times before - I would forget. Not the concept. The word. A simple, ordinary word that should have been right there. Or I would write a common spelling on the board and suddenly doubt whether it was correct. My hand would hover over the letters, my mind going blank, the students watching, and I would have to pretend I was just pausing for emphasis.

The depression was always there, a heavy fog I was walking through. But what I did not understand for a long time was how much of it was living in my body. The exhaustion that eight hours of sleep did not touch. The way my stomach would clench before each class, even after years of teaching. The headaches that came without obvious cause. The shoulder and neck tension that felt like I was carrying something heavy all the time - which, I suppose, I was.

But here is the strange thing. The students loved me. They remembered me. Years later, I would run into former students who would tell me I was one of the teachers who made a difference, who made them feel seen, who cared. And I did care. Intensely. Maybe too intensely. Because I was not just teaching them biology. I was trying, unconsciously, to get from them what I had never gotten as a child: connection. Warmth. The feeling of mattering to someone. I attached to them because I needed attachment. And they felt it - that genuine care, that investment in their success and wellbeing. They did not know it was also a kind of hunger.

This chapter is about what I did not understand then: that trauma does not live only in your thoughts or your memories or your emotions. It lives in your body. In your muscles, your digestive system, your immune response, your chronic pain. Long after the mind tries to move on, the body is still braced for impact. Still holding the tension of a danger that passed years ago. Still speaking in a language that most people - including the person living inside that body - do not know how to read.

6.1 - Psychoneuroimmunology: The Body Is Not Separate

There is a field of science with an intimidatingly long name - psychoneuroimmunology - that studies something beautifully simple: the nervous system, the endocrine system, and the immune system are not separate. They are one integrated communication network. What happens in your mind affects your body. What happens in your body affects your mind. And trauma, which arrives as a psychological experience, becomes a biological one.

For most of Western medical history, this was not understood. Or rather, it was understood intuitively by patients - who knew that stress made them sick, that grief could weaken them, that emotional distress showed up in their bodies - but it was not taken seriously by science. The mind was one domain. The body was another. Psychology studied the first. Medicine studied the second. And the two rarely spoke to each other.

That division was always artificial. And over the last few decades, the science has made it impossible to maintain. We now know, with precision and replicability, that psychological stress produces measurable changes in immune function. That chronic emotional distress alters inflammatory markers in the bloodstream. That early childhood adversity - the kind we have been talking about throughout this book - shows up decades later not just in mental health outcomes but in cardiovascular disease, autoimmune disorders, metabolic syndrome, and cancer rates.

The body keeps the score. That phrase - borrowed from Bessel van der Kolk's essential book on trauma - is not a metaphor. It is a description of how biology works.

The Bidirectional Highway: How Stress Becomes Inflammation

When you experience psychological stress - and childhood trauma counts as chronic psychological stress, even when it is no longer happening, because the stress-response system stays activated - your brain communicates that stress to the rest of your body through multiple pathways.

The HPA axis, which we have discussed before, releases cortisol. The sympathetic nervous system releases adrenaline and norepinephrine. And these stress hormones do not stay in the brain. They travel through the bloodstream to every organ, every tissue, every cell. And one of the things they do is activate the immune system.

Now, in the short term, this activation is useful. The immune system is preparing for potential injury, potential infection - because in the ancestral environment, stress usually meant physical danger, and physical danger often meant wounds that needed defending against bacteria and viruses. So the immune system ramps up its inflammatory response. It mobilizes white blood cells. It increases production of cytokines - signaling proteins that coordinate the immune response.

All of this is adaptive. For a short time. The problem, as with so much of the trauma response, is what happens when short-term becomes long-term. When the stress never fully resolves. When the HPA axis keeps signaling danger, and the immune system keeps responding, and the inflammation that was supposed to be temporary becomes chronic.

> *Chronic psychological stress produces chronic inflammation. And chronic inflammation is not just uncomfortable - it is one of the primary mechanisms through which trauma becomes physical disease.*

What Inflammation Actually Does to the Body

Inflammation is one of those words that gets used casually - we talk about foods being anti-inflammatory, about reducing inflammation through lifestyle changes - but I want to be specific about what we are actually talking about at the biological level.

Acute inflammation - the kind you get when you sprain an ankle or cut your hand - is characterized by redness, swelling, heat, and pain. Those are the visible signs of an immune response: blood flow increases to the area, white blood cells flood in, chemical signals coordinate the healing process. This is the body doing exactly what it is supposed to do. And when the injury heals, the inflammation resolves.

Chronic inflammation is different. It is low-grade, persistent, systemic. There is no visible swelling. No obvious injury being repaired. But at the cellular level, the immune system is in a constant state of mild activation. Pro-inflammatory cytokines - particularly interleukin-6, tumor necrosis factor-alpha, and C-reactive protein - circulate at elevated levels. And over time, this chronic activation causes damage.

It damages the endothelial cells lining blood vessels, contributing to atherosclerosis and cardiovascular disease. It interferes with insulin signaling, contributing to metabolic syndrome and type 2 diabetes. It promotes the growth of certain cancers. It accelerates the aging of cells, shortening telomeres - the protective caps on chromosomes - and quite literally making the body biologically older than its chronological age.

And in the brain - which is where this connects most directly to the previous chapters - chronic inflammation disrupts the production and function of neurotransmitters, interferes with neuroplasticity, and contributes to depression, anxiety, and cognitive decline.

This is not speculative. This is measurable. Adults with high ACE scores - high levels of childhood adversity - show elevated inflammatory markers decades after the adversity occurred. The childhood ended. The inflammation did not.

> *Research note: A 2017 study by Kuhlman and colleagues found that adults who experienced childhood maltreatment showed elevated levels of C-reactive protein - a key marker of systemic inflammation - even when*

> *controlling for current health behaviors like smoking, diet, and exercise. The inflammation was independent of current lifestyle. It was written into the biology by early experience and persisted into adulthood.*

6.2 - Chronic Pain, Illness, and the ACE Connection

Let me tell you about something that happened repeatedly during those eight years I spent teaching.

> I would get sick more often than my colleagues. Not dramatically - not hospitalized, not bedridden for weeks. Just the chronic low-level illnesses that accumulate. A cold that would knock me down for a week when others recovered in three days. Digestive problems that doctors could not quite explain - everything looked normal on tests, but my stomach disagreed. Headaches that were not quite migraines but were persistent enough to interfere. And fatigue. Always, always the fatigue, even on days when I had done nothing that should have made me tired.
>
> I assumed this was just how my body worked. Some people are healthier than others. I was in the unlucky category. What I did not understand - what nobody had ever told me - was that my body was not unlucky. It was responding. To a history. To a childhood that had asked my nervous system to stay on high alert for years, and to a nervous system that had never fully stood down.

The connection between childhood trauma and adult physical illness is one of the most robust findings in all of public health research. We touched on this in Chapter 2 when discussing the ACE Study, but I want to go deeper here, because the mechanism matters.

Fibromyalgia, IBS, and the Disorders That Medicine Cannot Quite Explain

There is a category of medical conditions that are frustrating for both patients and doctors because they are real - the symptoms are undeniable, the suffering is genuine - but the standard medical tests come back normal. No visible pathology. No infection. No structural damage. Just pain, or fatigue, or digestive chaos, or all of the above.

Fibromyalgia - widespread chronic pain and tenderness. Irritable bowel syndrome - abdominal pain, bloating, diarrhea or constipation with no detectable disease. Chronic fatigue syndrome - exhaustion so profound that ordinary activities become impossible. Interstitial cystitis - bladder pain without infection. Tension headaches and migraines that resist standard treatment.

For a long time, these conditions were dismissed as psychosomatic - meaning, essentially, imaginary. Not real illness, but anxiety manifesting as physical symptoms. This was both insulting to patients and scientifically wrong. The symptoms are not imaginary. The pain is not 'all in your head.' What is happening is that the pain is in the nervous system - in the way the nervous system processes and amplifies signals from the body - in ways that standard medical imaging cannot easily detect.

And here is the connection to trauma: all of these conditions - fibromyalgia, IBS, chronic fatigue, the whole constellation of what are sometimes called functional disorders or central sensitivity syndromes - show up at dramatically higher rates in people with histories of childhood adversity.

A person with an ACE score of four or higher is twice as likely to develop fibromyalgia, twice as likely to have chronic fatigue, and significantly more likely to have chronic digestive problems compared to someone with an ACE score of zero. This is not because trauma survivors are more likely to complain or less likely to tolerate discomfort. It is because the nervous system shaped by chronic early stress processes pain differently. The alarm system is sensitized. The threshold for what registers as painful is lower. The volume on bodily signals is turned up.

> *The body that learned to be hypervigilant does not stop being hypervigilant just because the danger is gone. It applies that same heightened sensitivity to everything - including the ordinary signals from muscles, joints, and organs that other nervous systems filter out.*

The Gut-Brain Axis: Why Trauma Shows Up in Your Stomach

There is a reason people say they have a gut feeling. A reason anxiety makes your stomach hurt. A reason stress gives you diarrhea or makes you nauseous. The gut and the brain are in constant communication, connected by something called the vagus nerve - a massive bundle of nerve fibers that runs from the brainstem down through the chest and abdomen, carrying signals in both directions.

About ninety percent of the signals traveling along the vagus nerve are going up - from the gut to the brain - not down. Your gut is sending information to your brain constantly, about the state of digestion, about the microbiome, about inflammation, about threat. And the brain responds by modulating gut function - speeding it up, slowing it down, changing motility and secretion and sensitivity based on what the brain interprets as the current level of danger.

In a person whose nervous system is chronically activated - whose brain is perpetually signaling some degree of threat - the gut receives those signals and responds accordingly. Motility becomes erratic. Inflammation increases. The balance of bacteria in the microbiome shifts toward species associated with anxiety and depression. The gut becomes a second site of the stress response, producing physical symptoms that often mystify both the patient and their doctor.

This is why so many trauma survivors have digestive problems that standard gastroenterology cannot fix. The problem is not in the gut alone. It is in the communication between the gut and a brain that is still, at some level, waiting for something terrible to happen.

> *I lived for years with what doctors vaguely called 'stress-related digestive issues.' Which was true but not helpful, because knowing that stress was the cause did not tell me how to stop being stressed. What I did not know then was that the stress was not situational. It was not about my job or my workload. It was embedded. It was the way my autonomic nervous system had learned to operate - chronically braced, chronically activated - and until that changed, the gut symptoms would continue. And they did.*

Autoimmune Disorders and the Body Attacking Itself

There is an entire category of disease in which the immune system - which is supposed to protect the body from foreign invaders - turns on the body's own tissues. Rheumatoid arthritis. Lupus. Multiple sclerosis. Type 1 diabetes. Hashimoto's thyroiditis. Psoriasis. Inflammatory bowel disease. The list is long and growing.

We do not fully understand what causes autoimmune disorders. Genetics plays a role. Environmental triggers play a role. But one factor that keeps showing up in the research is chronic stress, particularly early-life stress. And the mechanism, as with so much else, appears to be inflammation.

Chronic psychological stress produces chronic immune activation. Chronic immune activation increases the production of autoantibodies - antibodies that mistakenly target the body's own cells. The immune system, kept on high alert for so long, starts making errors. It starts attacking things it should not attack. And once that process begins, it tends to become self-perpetuating.

This is not to say that trauma causes autoimmune disease in any simple, direct way. But it creates the biological conditions in which autoimmune disease is more likely to develop. It shifts the odds. And for people already genetically predisposed, the chronic stress and inflammation of a traumatic childhood can be the environmental factor that tips the balance.

6.3 - The Vagus Nerve and the Polyvagal Theory

Stephen Porges, a neuroscientist whose work has transformed how we understand the nervous system's role in trauma and connection, developed something called polyvagal theory. And it is one of the most useful frameworks I know for making sense of why the body responds the way it does.

The vagus nerve, which I mentioned briefly in the previous section, is the longest nerve in the autonomic nervous system. It connects the brainstem to almost every major organ - heart, lungs, digestive tract - and it is the primary channel through which the brain regulates the body's basic functions without conscious thought.

What Porges discovered is that the vagus nerve is not a single system. It is two systems, evolutionarily distinct, that serve different functions and respond to different cues.

The Three States: Safety, Danger, and Shutdown

Polyvagal theory describes three basic states that the autonomic nervous system can be in, depending on what it perceives about the environment.

The first is the state of safety and social engagement. When the nervous system detects cues of safety - a calm voice, a warm face, predictable and gentle behavior from others - it activates what Porges calls the ventral vagal pathway. This is the most recently evolved part of the vagus system. It is uniquely mammalian. And what it does is beautiful: it relaxes the heart rate, deepens the breath, relaxes the muscles of the face and voice, and opens the body to connection. You can hear it in someone's voice - the warmth, the melodic quality, the expressiveness. You can see it in their face - the eyes that soften, the posture that opens. This is the state in which genuine connection happens. In which learning happens. In which the body feels safe enough to rest.

The second state is mobilization - fight or flight. When the nervous system detects danger, it activates the sympathetic system. Heart rate increases. Breathing quickens. Blood flow shifts to the muscles. Digestion shuts down. The body prepares to run or to fight. This is adaptive for acute threat. This is what keeps you alive when something is genuinely trying to hurt you. But it is not a state you are meant to live in.

The third state - and this is the one that surprised many researchers when Porges first described it - is shutdown. When the threat is inescapable, when fighting and fleeing have both failed or are impossible, the nervous system does something ancient and desperate: it shuts down. This is the dorsal vagal pathway, the oldest part of the vagus system, shared with reptiles. It slows the heart, drops blood pressure, produces a kind of numbing dissociation. In extreme cases, it is what produces fainting. In chronic cases, it is what produces the profound, exhausted immobility that so many trauma survivors recognize as depression.

> *The body has three responses to threat: connect and calm, mobilize and fight, or shut down and disappear. Trauma survivors often get stuck between the second and third - too activated to rest, too shut down to engage.*

Neuroception: The Unconscious Detection of Safety and Danger

Porges introduced another concept that is essential for understanding trauma and the body: neuroception. This is not a typo. It is different from perception, which is conscious awareness. Neuroception is the nervous system's automatic, unconscious evaluation of whether the environment is safe, dangerous, or life-threatening.

Your nervous system is scanning constantly - reading faces, listening to tone of voice, tracking movements, sensing the quality of silence in a room. And it is making decisions about which state to be in based on that scan, all without your conscious awareness. This is why you can walk into a room and immediately feel uneasy, even though nothing overtly threatening has happened. Your neuroception picked up something. Some cue that resembled danger.

For people with trauma histories, neuroception is often miscalibrated. The system learned to detect threat in an environment where threat was common. And it continues to detect threat - in neutral faces, in ordinary conversations, in situations that are objectively safe - because the detection system was trained in a world where safety was rare.

This is why trauma survivors often feel anxious or shut down in situations that do not, by any objective measure, warrant it. The conscious mind knows there is no danger. But the autonomic nervous system - running its neuroceptive scan, comparing the present environment to the library of past environments, finding resemblances to threat - activates anyway. And once it activates, no amount of rational thought will deactivate it. You cannot think your way out of a nervous system state. The body has to feel safe, not just think safe.

> *In the classroom, I could feel this happen. Some days I would walk in and my nervous system would be in ventral vagal mode - calm, open, connected. I could engage with the students easily, make jokes, respond flexibly to questions. Other days, for reasons I could not consciously identify, I would be in sympathetic activation*

> *- heart rate slightly elevated, jaw tight, a low hum of anxiety even though nothing was wrong. And on the worst days, I would be in dorsal shutdown - going through the motions, my voice flat, feeling like I was watching myself teach from somewhere far away. The students noticed. I could see it in their faces. But I did not know then that this was my autonomic nervous system cycling through states based on cues I could not consciously perceive.*

The Possibility of Re-Regulation

Here is the hope in polyvagal theory. The nervous system states are not fixed. They are responsive to environment. They were shaped by experience - by the particular environments of childhood - and they can be reshaped by new experience.

This happens slowly. It happens through what Porges calls co-regulation - the process by which one person's regulated nervous system helps regulate another's. An infant co-regulates with a calm caregiver. An adult can co-regulate with a therapist, a partner, a friend whose presence communicates safety. Over time, with enough experiences of safe connection, the neuroceptive system begins to recalibrate. It begins to recognize cues of safety more readily. The ventral vagal state becomes more accessible.

This is not a quick process. The nervous system is conservative. It does not change its threat-detection settings easily. But it does change. The body that learned to brace can learn, eventually, to unbrace. We will return to this in Part Three, when we talk about what healing actually looks like in practice.

6.4 - Reclaiming the Body

For many people who grew up with trauma, the body is not experienced as a home. It is experienced as a site of betrayal - the place where pain happened, where control was taken, where the self was violated or overwhelmed. The natural response to this is to dissociate from the body. To live primarily in the head. To treat the body as something to manage and control rather than something to inhabit.

And for a long time, that strategy works well enough. You can get through most of life by being smart, being competent, being useful - by living in the realm of thought and accomplishment and leaving the body to do its basic functions without much attention. Until it stops working. Until the body starts sending signals that cannot be ignored: pain, illness, exhaustion, the somatic symptoms that insist on being felt.

This is when people often first encounter the idea that healing trauma requires coming back into the body. And that idea can feel strange, counterintuitive, even threatening. Why would you want to feel more of what the body has to say, when what it has been saying is discomfort, pain, and the activation of old fear?

The answer - and this is something I had to learn through direct experience, not just intellectual understanding - is that the body is not just carrying the wound. It is also carrying the capacity to heal. The body knows how to regulate, how to come back to baseline, how to release tension and return to safety. It has just forgotten. Or rather, it never learned, because the environment never allowed it.

Somatic Therapies: When Talking Is Not Enough

Traditional talk therapy - sitting in a room, describing your experiences, gaining insight into patterns - is enormously valuable for many things. It helps people make sense of their stories. It provides relationship and witnessing. It offers cognitive tools for managing thoughts and emotions.

But for trauma that lives primarily in the body - for the chronic pain, the digestive problems, the dissociation, the nervous system stuck in fight-or-flight or shutdown - talking is often not enough. Because the trauma is not stored as narrative. It is stored as sensation, as muscle tension, as autonomic activation. And accessing it requires working directly with the body.

This is where somatic therapies come in. Approaches like Somatic Experiencing, Sensorimotor Psychotherapy, EMDR (which includes a body-based component), and trauma-informed yoga all work with the body directly. They teach people to track sensations, to notice where activation lives in the body, to complete the defensive responses that were interrupted during trauma, and to gradually increase the nervous system's tolerance for feeling without becoming overwhelmed.

What these approaches recognize is that the body has its own memory, its own intelligence, and its own pathway to resolution. The chronic tension in your shoulders is not random. It is holding something. The knot in your stomach when you face a particular kind of situation is not irrational. It is carrying information. And learning to listen to those bodily signals - not to suppress them, not to override them, but to be curious about them - is often the beginning of being able to release them.

> *Research note: A 2014 study by van der Kolk and colleagues found that trauma-sensitive yoga produced significant reductions in PTSD symptoms - comparable to traditional psychotherapy - particularly for symptoms that involved bodily activation and dissociation. The mechanism appeared to be increased interoceptive awareness: the ability to sense what is happening inside the body and to tolerate those sensations without immediately needinq to escape them.*

Movement, Breath, and the Language the Body Speaks

One of the simplest and most powerful ways to work with a dysregulated nervous system is through movement and breath. Not exercise in the conventional sense - though that can help - but mindful, intentional movement that brings awareness to sensation and allows the body to discharge activation.

Shaking, for instance. Animals do this instinctively after a threat passes - they shake, they tremor, they discharge the adrenaline and cortisol that flooded their system during the freeze response. Humans, in our over-civilized way, tend to suppress this. We hold still. We compose ourselves. And the activation stays trapped.

Breathwork - particularly techniques that emphasize slow, deep breathing - directly activates the parasympathetic nervous system. It signals to the body: we are safe. There is no emergency. It is okay to rest. This is not just relaxation as a nice idea. It is a direct intervention in the physiology of the stress response.

Dance, gentle stretching, walking in nature, any form of movement that you do with attention rather than on autopilot - all of these help the body return to a sense of aliveness and presence that chronic trauma often suppresses.

> *I discovered this by accident. During one particularly dark period, when the depression was heavy and the dissociation was constant, I started walking. Not for exercise. Just to move. And I noticed that when I walked - particularly when I walked outside, in sports complex khurrianwala, where there were trees and quiet - something in me loosened. Not dramatically. Not a cure. But a small easing. A sense of being slightly more present in my body, slightly less trapped in my head. It was the first time I understood that the body could be part of the solution, not just the site of the problem.*

The Radical Act of Inhabiting Yourself

Reclaiming the body is not a single event. It is a practice. A long, slow, sometimes frustrating practice of learning to be present in a body that has not always been a safe place to be present

It means learning to notice sensation without immediately interpreting it as danger. To feel your heart rate increase and recognize it as just heart rate, not proof that something is wrong. To track the movement of breath in your chest, the weight of your body in a chair, the contact of your feet on the ground - small acts of attention that, repeated over time, begin to build a different relationship with embodiment

And it means, eventually, treating the body with the kindness and respect it deserves. Not as a machine to be pushed through fatigue. Not as something broken that needs fixing. But as the organism that has been carrying you through all of this. The one that kept you alive when you were a child in an impossible situation. The one that is still here, still trying, still capable of rest and pleasure and connection if given the right conditions.

> *Your body is not the enemy. It is the thing that survived. And learning to live in it again - fully, presently, without the dissociation or the bracing - is one of the most important kinds of healing there is.*

✦✦✦

I want to close this chapter by saying something to anyone who has spent years living primarily in their head, who has treated the body as an inconvenience or a betrayal, who has pushed through fatigue and pain and numbness without stopping to ask what the body might be trying to say.

I understand why you did that. The body was not always safe to inhabit. The signals it sent were overwhelming, or they reminded you of things you needed to forget, or they simply hurt too much to feel. Dissociation was not a choice. It was survival. And it worked, for a long time.

But there comes a point - and you may be at that point now, if you are reading this chapter - where the cost of staying disconnected from the body becomes higher than the cost of reconnecting. Where the chronic pain, the illness, the exhaustion, the sense of being a ghost in your own life, all become unbearable in a way that even the fear of feeling cannot match.

The body is still here. It has been waiting. It has been sending signals - some of them uncomfortable, some of them painful - not because it wants to hurt you, but because it wants to be heard. To be felt. To be allowed, finally, to rest.

Listening to it - learning its language, attending to its needs, offering it the safety and care it never received - is not a quick process. But it is a possible one. And the body, unlike the mind, does not hold grudges. It does not care how long you ignored it. It just wants to come home. And it is waiting for you to let it.

The Body Remembers - and the Body Can Heal

We have walked through some heavy territory in this chapter. The science of psychoneuroimmunology and how psychological stress becomes physical illness. Chronic pain and the disorders that medicine struggles to explain. The vagus nerve and polyvagal theory and why the body cycles through states of safety, danger, and shutdown. And the possibility - the genuine, science-backed possibility - of reclaiming a body that trauma taught you to leave.

What I hope you take from this is not a sense of being damaged, but a sense of being understood. The pain is real. The illness is real. The fatigue, the digestive chaos, the chronic tension - all of it is real, and all of it makes sense. The body is not broken. It is responding. To a history. To a nervous system shaped by conditions that required hypervigilance and bracing and constant readiness for threat.

And because the body is responding - not broken, but responding - it can learn to respond differently. The nervous system that learned one pattern can learn another. The muscles that learned to hold can learn to release. The immune system that learned to stay activated can learn to stand down.

This is not a promise of easy healing or quick recovery. The body's timescale is slow. Its changes are incremental. But they are real. And they are worth pursuing. Not because you owe it to anyone else, but because you deserve to live in a body that feels like ho
me.

☒ *Chapter 7: The Masks We Learn to Wear*

7

The Masks We Learn to Wear

Performance, Persona, and the Exhausting Art of Surviving Socially

"The mask is not a lie. It is the only face that was safe to show."

Let me tell you about a skill you probably developed without realizing you were developing it.

You walk into a room - a party, a meeting, a family gathering - and before you have consciously processed anything, you have already scanned the emotional temperature. Who is tense. Who is relaxed. Who is performing happiness and who actually feels it. Which conversations are safe to enter and which ones to avoid. The subtle shift in someone's tone that means danger, or annoyance, or that you have said something wrong even though they are still smiling.

You do this automatically. Effortlessly. You have been doing it since you were a child, because in the house you grew up in, survival required it. Reading the room was not a social nicety. It was intelligence gathering. Knowing when to speak and when to disappear, when to be helpful and when to be invisible, when to perform enthusiasm and when to mirror someone else's mood - these were not optional skills. They were the difference between a night that went smoothly and a night that did not.

And so you got very, very good at it. At reading people. At adjusting yourself to the room. At becoming whatever the situation required. You became - though no one ever named it this way - a masterful performer of social survival.

This chapter is about that performance. About the masks we learn to wear when the authentic self is not safe to show. About the extraordinary social intelligence that trauma survivors develop - and the extraordinary cost of using it constantly, in every interaction, with no rest. About what happens when you have spent so long being what others need that you no longer know what you are when no one is watching.

7.1 - The Hypervigilant Child: Reading Rooms Before Entering Them

Children are phenomenally good at learning what they need to learn to survive. And if what they need to learn is how to predict the unpredictable - how to sense danger before it fully materializes - they will learn that with an efficiency that rivals any formal education.

This is hypervigilance, which we have touched on in earlier chapters but which I want to examine here specifically in its social dimension. Because hypervigilance is not just about scanning for physical threat. It is about scanning for emotional threat. For the subtle cues that tell you whether this person is safe, whether this moment is safe, whether what you just said or did has changed the temperature in a way that will cost you something.

The Neuroscience of Social Threat Detection

The brain has specialized systems for processing social information. The fusiform face area, which recognizes faces with extraordinary speed and precision. The superior temporal sulcus, which reads intention from movement and gaze direction. The amygdala, which we have discussed extensively, but which is not just a fear detector - it is also a social salience detector, flagging faces and voices and behaviors that might signal threat or safety.

In a typical brain, these systems operate in the background, processing social information efficiently but not obtrusively.

You walk into a room, you recognize familiar faces, you orient toward friendly ones, you engage. The scanning happens, but it does not dominate consciousness.

In a brain shaped by an unpredictable or threatening social environment - which is what a chaotic or abusive home is - these systems become overdeveloped. They run constantly, at high sensitivity, with the volume turned way up. Every facial expression is scrutinized for signs of danger. Every pause in conversation is analyzed for what it might mean. Every shift in body language is registered and interpreted, often correctly, sometimes with false positives, but always with the underlying assumption that missing a threat would be worse than seeing threats that are not there.

This is adaptive. In the environment where it developed, this heightened sensitivity kept the child safe. It allowed them to avoid conflict, to read a parent's mood before stepping into danger, to modulate their own behavior in ways that minimized harm. The hypervigilant child is not anxious for no reason. They are anxious because anxiety, in their world, was information. And the information was often accurate.

> *The child who learned to read a room before entering it did not develop a disorder. They developed a survival skill. The problem is that the skill does not turn off when the danger is gone.*

The Adult Legacy: When Every Room Is a Test

The adult who grew up hypervigilant does not lose the skill. They carry it into every social situation, often without realizing they are doing it. And in some contexts - work, teaching, leadership, any role that requires managing people or navigating complex social dynamics - it can be an extraordinary asset. Trauma survivors are often unusually good at reading others, at anticipating needs, at managing group dynamics, precisely because they have spent their entire lives practicing.

But there is a cost. And the cost is exhaustion.

Imagine running a program in the background of your computer that is constantly scanning every file, every process, every piece of incoming data for potential threats. It works. It keeps you safe. But it also drains the battery constantly, slows down other processes, and uses resources that could have been allocated elsewhere. That is what social hypervigilance does to a person. It is running all the time, in every interaction, consuming energy that is not consciously noticed until you get home and realize you are completely drained from a social event that should have been enjoyable.

> *You go to a dinner party. You are friendly, engaging, appropriately interested in other people. You laugh at the right moments. You ask the right questions. From the outside, you look relaxed. But inside, you are working. You are tracking who is comfortable and who is not, who might be upset by what you just said, whether you*

> *have been talking too much or too little, whether the silence that just fell was comfortable or awkward. You are performing ease while monitoring for threat. And when you get home, you collapse. Not because anything bad happened. But because the vigilance itself is the cost.*

The Strange Gift: Emotional Intelligence Born from Necessity

There is something I want to name clearly, because it gets missed in discussions of trauma: the social intelligence that develops in response to an unpredictable environment is real intelligence. It is not compensation for damage. It is a genuine cognitive and emotional capacity that many people who grew up in safer circumstances simply do not have.

Trauma survivors are often extraordinarily empathic - not in the vague feel-good sense, but in the precise neurological sense of being able to read and respond to others' emotional states with unusual accuracy. They are often excellent therapists, teachers, caregivers, managers - roles that require the ability to sense what someone else is feeling before that person has fully articulated it.

This is not a silver lining. The cost was too high, and no child should have to pay it. But it is real. And for many trauma survivors, recognizing that the hypervigilance that exhausts them is also a capacity that serves them - that makes them good at things that matter - is important. Not because it justifies what happened, but because it honors what they built in response to it.

7.2 - Goffman's Dramaturgical Self

In 1959, sociologist Erving Goffman published a book called 'The Presentation of Self in Everyday Life,' and in it he argued something that was both obvious and radical: all social life is performance. We are always, to some degree, playing a role. Managing impressions. Adjusting our behavior to fit the situation and the audience.

Goffman called this the dramaturgical model of social interaction. He distinguished between front stage - the public performance, the self we show to others - and back stage - the private self, the place where we drop the performance and can be unguarded. And he argued that this is universal. Everyone does it. The waiter who is polite to customers but complains about them in the kitchen. The professional who maintains composure in meetings but relaxes at home. This is not deception. It is simply how social life works.

But for people who grew up in traumatic environments, the dramaturgical model hits differently. Because what Goffman is describing as a normal feature of social life - the performance, the mask, the adjustment of self to context - is not something they do occasionally in formal settings. It is something they do constantly, in almost every context, because not performing was never safe.

When There Is No Back Stage

Goffman's model assumes that everyone has a back stage - a place where the performance can drop, where you can be unguarded, where the authentic self can emerge without consequence. For most people, that place is home. Family. Close friends. The contexts where you do not have to manage impressions because the people present already know you and accept you.

But what happens when home was the front stage? When family was the audience that required the most careful performance? When even in private, you had to manage someone else's emotions, monitor for danger, present a version of yourself that would not provoke or disappoint or trigger rage?

Then there is no back stage. Or rather, the back stage is so small - maybe just the inside of your own head, and even there not reliably - that you never fully learn what it feels like to drop the mask. The performance becomes so constant, so totalizing, that it stops feeling like performance. It just feels like existing. And the question 'who are you when you are not performing?' becomes almost unanswerable, because you have so little experience of not performing that you genuinely do not know.

> *The mask you wore to survive was not a disguise. It was the face that kept you safe. And wearing it for long enough, you can forget what you looked like underneath.*

The Impostor Phenomenon and the Performed Self

There is a psychological phenomenon called impostor syndrome - the persistent feeling that you are a fraud, that your accomplishments are not real, that at any moment someone will discover that you do not actually belong in the position you hold. It is common in high-achieving individuals, particularly those from marginalized groups, and it has been studied extensively.

But I want to suggest that for trauma survivors, impostor syndrome is not quite the right framework. Because the feeling is not 'I am not as competent as people think.' It is deeper than that. It is 'I am not who people think I am. The person they are interacting with is a performance. And if they knew what I actually am - anxious, exhausted, barely holding it together, fundamentally different from the composed self I show them - they would not want me here.'

This is not an irrational belief. It is an accurate description of a real experience. The public self is a performance. The private self is struggling. And the gap between them is enormous. The fear is not that you will be exposed as incompetent. It is that you will be exposed as performing - and that once people see the performance for what it is, they will reject the person underneath.

What makes this particularly painful is that often, the person underneath the performance is more interesting, more genuine, more worthy of connection than the performed version. But the performed version is what feels safe. So you keep performing, even as the performance exhausts you, even as the distance between the mask and the face grows, because the alternative - being seen as you actually are - feels too risky.

7.3 - The Closet as Metaphor and Reality

I want to talk about a specific form of mask-wearing that carries its own particular weight: the closet. The experience of hiding a fundamental aspect of your identity - your sexuality, your gender, any core truth about who you are - because the world you inhabit is not safe for that truth.

For many trauma survivors, the closet is not an abstract concept. It is a lived experience. And for those who are both trauma survivors and queer - carrying both the wounds of childhood adversity and the need to conceal a fundamental identity - the compounding is profound. Because you are not just performing a social self. You are performing a straight self. Or a cisgender self. Or whatever version of yourself the world has told you is acceptable. And that performance is happening on top of all the other performances, all the other masks, all the other adjustments you already learned to make to stay safe.

The Double Bind: Hiding the Wound and Hiding the Self

There is something uniquely exhausting about carrying multiple concealments at once. You are hiding the trauma - the depression, the history, the reasons you sometimes struggle in ways other people do not. And you are hiding your identity - the part of you that knows, quietly and with increasing certainty, that you are not what others assume you to be.

And these two forms of hiding reinforce each other. The trauma taught you that authenticity is dangerous. That showing vulnerability invites harm. That the real you - whatever that is - is not safe to reveal. And then the closet teaches you the same lesson all over again: that the truth about who you are will cost you something. That the world is safer when you perform what it expects. That the mask is not optional.

The result is a kind of compounded invisibility. You are not seen as wounded, because you have learned to hide that. And you are not seen as queer, because you have learned to hide that too. And the exhaustion of maintaining both performances simultaneously, of monitoring constantly which truths can be spoken and which cannot, of code-switching not just between professional and personal contexts but between the self you show and the self you are - that exhaustion becomes the baseline. The water you swim in. The thing you do not even notice anymore because you have been doing it for so long.

> *When you have to hide who you are and what you carry, you do not just lose the ability to be seen. You lose the ability to see yourself clearly. The mask becomes the mirror.*

Coming Out: The Radical Act of Dropping One Mask

Coming out - in whatever form it takes, to whatever audience - is often described as liberating. And it can be. But for trauma survivors, coming out is also terrifying in a very specific way, because it requires doing the thing that trauma taught you never to do: making yourself vulnerable. Showing a truth about yourself that others might reject. Trusting that the consequences of authenticity will not destroy you.

And here is what often happens. You come out - to a friend, to family, to the world - and the response is... fine. Better than you expected. Sometimes even supportive. And you feel relief. And also, strangely, grief. Because if it was always going to be okay, why did you spend so long hiding? Why did the fear feel so real?

The answer, of course, is that the fear was real. It was trained into you by a childhood that taught you that authenticity had consequences. And even if coming out goes well - even if the world receives you with kindness - the nervous system that learned to hide does not immediately unlearn that lesson. It takes time. It takes repeated experiences of being seen and not harmed. It takes a slow, gradual recalibration of the threat-detection system to recognize that this truth, at least, is safe to tell.

And for many people, coming out is just the beginning of a longer process: learning to stop performing altogether. To stop modulating your voice, your mannerisms, your presentation based on who is in the room. To stop hiding the other things - the trauma, the struggle, the messy interior reality - that you learned to conceal long before you learned to conceal your queerness. Coming out of one closet often reveals the presence of others. And each one requires its own work, its own courage, its own slow process of learning that being seen will not kill you.

7.4 - People-Pleasing, Fawning, and the Trauma Response Nobody Talks About

You have probably heard of fight or flight. The sympathetic nervous system's two primary responses to threat: mobilize to fight, or mobilize to flee. And in recent decades, freeze has been added to the list - the parasympathetic shutdown response when fight and flight are both impossible.

But there is a fourth response that gets much less attention, even though it is extraordinarily common in people with trauma histories. It is called fawn. And if you recognize yourself in this chapter, if you have spent your life reading rooms and adjusting yourself to others and performing whatever the situation requires, this is probably the trauma response you know best.

What Fawning Actually Is

Fawning is the attempt to neutralize threat through appeasement. Through making yourself useful, agreeable, pleasant, helpful, non-threatening. Through prioritizing the other person's needs and emotions over your own. Through becoming whatever they need you to be so that they will not hurt you.

It develops most often in situations where fight and flight are not options. A child cannot fight a parent. A child cannot flee a home. But a child can learn to be good. To be helpful. To be easy. To anticipate needs before they are voiced and meet them before they become demands. To smile when they are scared, to agree when they disagree, to shrink themselves to fit whatever space is available, to make themselves so indispensable or so inoffensive that harm becomes less likely.

And it works. Not always, but often enough that the pattern gets reinforced. The child learns: aggression invites aggression, resistance invites punishment, but compliance - exaggerated, proactive, relentless compliance - can sometimes create safety. Or at least reduce danger.

> *Fawning is not weakness. It is not cowardice. It is the choice your nervous system made when the alternatives were worse. And like every trauma response, it made sense in the moment - and costs something in the long run.*

The Adult Fawn Response: People-Pleasing as Nervous System State

In adulthood, fawning shows up as chronic people-pleasing. As difficulty saying no. As the automatic impulse to make others comfortable even at the expense of your own comfort. As taking on responsibilities that are not yours, managing other people's emotions, apologizing for things you did not do, and feeling responsible for others' reactions to you.

It looks, from the outside, like being nice. Agreeable. Helpful. Easygoing. And these can be genuine virtues. But when they are compulsive - when you cannot not do them, when the thought of disappointing someone or being disliked produces a visceral panic, when you find yourself saying yes to things you do not want to do and apologizing for existing in a space - then they are not virtues. They are a nervous system stuck in a defensive response that was learned long ago and never fully deactivated.

> *You are in a meeting. Someone proposes an idea you think is flawed. You have the expertise to know it will not work. But you do not say anything. Or if you do, you frame your objection so carefully, so gently, with so much deference to the other person's perspective, that the criticism is nearly invisible. Because disagreeing feels dangerous. Because being perceived as difficult, or critical, or not a team player - these feel like existential threats, even though intellectually you know they are not. The fawn response does not care about your intellect. It cares about keeping you safe. And in the world where it learned its job, disagreeing was not safe.*

The Hidden Cost: Resentment and Self-Erasure

One of the most painful aspects of chronic fawning is that it generates resentment. Not immediately. Not consciously. But over time, as you keep prioritizing others' needs over your own, as you keep shrinking yourself to make space for others, as you keep giving more than you have and receiving less than you need - the resentment accumulates. Quietly. Invisibly.

Until one day you realize you are angry at the people you have been trying so hard to please.

And the cruelest part is that often, they did not ask for it. They did not demand that you ignore your own needs, or agree when you disagreed, or take care of them at your own expense. You did that. Your nervous system did that. Because it learned, a long time ago, that this was how you stayed safe.

So you are angry at them for accepting what you offered. And you are angry at yourself for offering it. And underneath all of that is the original wound: the learning, early and thorough, that your needs do not matter as much as keeping others happy. That your worth is measured by your usefulness. That love is something you earn through service, not something you receive just for existing.

Learning to Disappoint: The Hardest Skill

If fawning is the automatic response, then learning not to fawn requires learning one of the most difficult skills a trauma survivor can learn: the ability to disappoint people and survive it.

To say no. To disagree. To prioritize your own needs even when doing so inconveniences someone else. To let someone be upset with you without immediately trying to fix it. To tolerate the discomfort of being disliked, or disappointing someone, or failing to meet an expectation - without collapsing into panic or shame.

This is not a skill you learn by deciding to learn it. It is a skill you learn by doing the thing that feels dangerous - saying no, disagreeing, prioritizing yourself - and discovering, slowly and with many repetitions, that the catastrophe you feared does not happen. That most people are more resilient than your nervous system believes. That disappointing someone does not end the relationship. That being less than perfectly agreeable does not result in abandonment or harm.

It is slow work. It is uncomfortable work. And it requires, often, the support of people who can tolerate your first awkward attempts at setting boundaries without punishing you for them. But it is possible. The nervous system that learned to fawn can learn, eventually, that there are other ways to be safe.

✦✦✦

I want to close this section by saying something directly to anyone who recognized themselves in the description of fawning.

You are not weak. You are not a doormat. You are not pathologically nice or lacking in self-respect. You are a person whose nervous system learned, under conditions of genuine danger, to keep you safe by making you useful and agreeable and non-threatening. And that strategy worked. It kept you alive. It got you through a childhood that required it.

The fact that it is costing you something now - the exhaustion, the resentment, the sense of having disappeared into the needs of others - does not mean you were wrong to develop it. It means you are ready to outgrow it. To learn a different way of being safe. One that does not require erasing yourself.

And that is possible. Not quickly. Not without discomfort. But genuinely, it is possible. The person you were performing for others is not who you have to keep being. You are allowed to take up space. To have needs. To say no. To be, occasionally, difficult. And the people worth keeping in your life will not leave when you stop performing. They will be relieved to finally meet you.

The Mask Was Necessary - And Now It Can Come Off

We have covered a lot of ground in this chapter. The hyper-vigilance that makes you unusually good at reading people - and unusually exhausted by social interaction. Goffman's dramaturgical self and what happens when there is no back stage, no place where the performance can drop. The closet as both metaphor and reality, and the particular exhaustion of hiding both trauma and identity simultaneously. And fawning - the fourth trauma response, the one that shows up as chronic people-pleasing and that so many trauma survivors carry without ever being told it has a name.

What I want you to take from this chapter is not shame about the masks you wear. The masks were necessary. They kept you safe in situations where safety required performance. They are evidence of your intelligence, your adaptability, your capacity to do what was needed under difficult circumstances.

But the fact that the masks were necessary does not mean they have to be permanent. The social intelligence you developed - the capacity to read people, to navigate complex dynamics, to manage others' emotions - that is real, and it is valuable.

What you are working toward is not losing that intelligence. It is learning when to use it and when to put it down. Learning that you do not have to perform in every context, with every person, all the time. That there are places and people with whom the authentic self - uncertain, imperfect, sometimes difficult - is safe to show.

The mask is not you. But it has been your face for so long that taking it off feels dangerous. Like exposing something raw. Like standing in a room without armor. And that feeling is real, and it is hard, and it deserves to be acknowledged.

But underneath the mask is a face. A real one. The one that was always there, waiting. And it is worth the discomfort of revealing. Not to everyone. Not all at once. But slowly, carefully, with people who have earned the right to see it. The world does not need another performance. It needs you. The actual you. The one who is tired of performing and ready, finally, to be seen.

⊠ *Chapter 8: Money, Class, and the Wounds That Work Inflicts*

8

Money, Class, and the Wounds That Work Inflicts

Poverty, Labor, and the Economics of Surviving Without a Safety Net

"There is a particular loneliness in working hard for what others receive as birthright."

When I was in college, my father decided he would no longer pay my tuition. The reason was never entirely clear - or rather, the reasons changed depending on when you asked. Sometimes it was about money. Sometimes it was about teaching me a lesson. Sometimes it was punishment for something I had or had not done. But the reason did not matter as much as the consequence: I needed to stay in school, and I had no money to do it.

So I worked. Part-time jobs that became full-time hours.

Labor jobs, mostly. Construction. Loading docks. The kind of work where your body is the tool and you are paid by the hour and you go home aching in ways that make sleep difficult and waking up harder. I was studying biology while my hands were raw from concrete and my back was complaining about lifting things it was not designed to lift repeatedly.

I look back on those years now and feel a strange mix of pride and grief. Pride because I did it - I made it through, I got the education, I became a teacher. And grief because I should not have had to. Because there were other students in my classes whose parents paid their tuition as a matter of course, who had never had to choose between working enough hours to eat and attending enough classes to pass, who got to spend their college years actually being college students rather than exhausted laborers trying to stay awake during lectures.

This chapter is about money, and class, and the particular wounds that economic adversity inflicts. Not as a political tract - though the politics matter - but as a psychological and biological reality. Because money is not just money. It is access, opportunity, stress, safety, health, and time. And growing up without it, or having it withheld as punishment, or needing it desperately and working yourself into exhaustion to get it - these experiences do something to a person. They shape not just your bank account but your nervous system, your sense of worth, your relationship to work and rest and deserving.

8.1 - Poverty and the Brain: What Scarcity Does to Cognition

There is a book by economists Sendhil Mullainathan and Eldar Shafir called 'Scarcity: Why Having Too Little Means So Much,' and it contains one of the most important insights I have encountered about what poverty actually does to human cognition. Their central argument is simple and devastating: scarcity captures attention.

When you do not have enough of something critical - money, time, food, safety - your brain becomes preoccupied with that lack. Not because you are weak-willed or short-sighted, but because scarcity is genuinely urgent. The question 'how will I pay rent?' or 'where will my next meal come from?' or 'can I afford to get sick?' is not a background concern you can table until later. It is an immediate problem demanding cognitive resources right now. And those resources - attention, working memory, executive function - are finite. When they are occupied by managing scarcity, they are not available for other things.

The Bandwidth Tax

Mullainathan and Shafir call this the bandwidth tax. Poverty does not just reduce your financial resources. It reduces your cognitive bandwidth. It is like trying to use a computer while running multiple resource-intensive programs in the background. The computer still works, but it is slower. Applications take longer to load. Multitasking becomes difficult. And this is not because the processor is defective. It is because the processor is busy.

The same thing happens in the human brain under conditions of scarcity. People living in poverty show measurably reduced performance on cognitive tasks - not because they are less intelligent, but because a significant portion of their cognitive capacity is occupied by the mental arithmetic of survival. How much is in the bank. How much is owed. How to stretch what is left until the next paycheck. Whether to buy food or pay the heating bill. Whether to risk the late fee or the overdraft charge.

And this matters enormously for understanding why poverty is so hard to escape. It is not just that poor people make bad decisions. It is that poverty makes decision-making harder. The bandwidth required to plan long-term, to invest in education, to avoid expensive mistakes - all of that is taxed by the immediate cognitive load of managing scarcity.

> *Poverty does not just deprive you of resources. It occupies your mind, constantly, with the exhausting work of not having enough. And that occupation makes everything else - school, work, relationships, health - harder than it should be.*

Childhood Poverty and the Developing Brain

If scarcity taxes cognitive bandwidth in adults, imagine what it does to a developing child. A child whose family is struggling financially is not just experiencing material deprivation. They are growing up in a home where stress is chronic, where uncertainty is constant, where the adults are preoccupied with problems that children cannot fully understand but can absolutely sense.

The research on childhood poverty and brain development is clear and sobering. Children who grow up in poverty show measurable differences in brain structure and function compared to their more affluent peers. The prefrontal cortex - responsible for executive function, impulse control, planning - develops more slowly. The hippocampus, which we have discussed extensively in earlier chapters, shows reduced volume. The amygdala, the threat-detection system, is larger and more reactive.

These are not genetic differences. They are environmental. The brain is adapting to the conditions it is growing up in. And the conditions of poverty - the chronic stress, the unpredictability, the lack of enriching experiences, the parental stress that reduces the quality of caregiving - shape the developing brain in ways that make academic achievement, emotional regulation, and future economic success all statistically less likely.

This is not determinism. Many people who grow up in poverty overcome these disadvantages through a combination of individual effort, supportive relationships, and sheer resilience. But it is harder. Measurably, consistently, predictably harder. And pretending otherwise does not honor the reality of what poverty asks of people.

Research note: A 2015 study by Hair and colleagues found that family income-to-needs ratio was significantly associated with children's brain development, with the largest effects in areas supporting language, reading, executive function, and spatial skills. The relationship was particularly strong at the lower end of the income spectrum - meaning that the difference between dire poverty and modest poverty mattered more, neurologically, than the difference between middle class and wealthy.

8.2 - The Dignity of Working with Your Hands

I want to pause here and say something that the research on poverty sometimes misses, because it is focused on deficits and difficulties and what poverty does to people. Which is all true and important. But there is another side to working-class life and manual labor that deserves to be named, because it is real and it matters and it shaped me in ways I am still discovering.

Working with your hands teaches you things that no amount of formal education can. It teaches you the relationship between effort and result - you lift the thing, you move the thing, the thing is moved. There is a clarity to that feedback loop that is often absent in intellectual work, where the effort you put in and the outcome you get are mediated by so many variables that the connection can feel arbitrary. Manual labor is not arbitrary. It is concrete. Literal. The work is visible and the day's accomplishment is undeniable.

Shop Class as Soulcraft: The Knowledge in Your Hands

There is a book by philosopher and mechanic Matthew Crawford called 'Shop Class as Soulcraft,' and it argues something that academic culture often resists: that skilled manual work is a form of intelligence. A welder knows things that cannot be expressed in propositions. A carpenter understands structural integrity in ways that are embodied, tactile, learned through thousands of repetitions. A cook knows when the sauce is ready not because they have memorized a temperature but because they have developed a feel for it.

This kind of knowledge is real knowledge. It is not less sophisticated than theoretical knowledge - it is differently sophisticated. And for people who have had access to both - who have worked with their hands and also worked with ideas - there is often a recognition that the physical work provided something the intellectual work could not: a sense of competence that is immediate, verifiable, and grounded in reality.

> *When I was working construction to pay for college, I hated it. The hours. The exhaustion. The way my body hurt. But there was also something I did not expect: a satisfaction. At the end of a shift, you could look at what you had built. A wall that was not there in the morning. A foundation that was poured and smoothed and would be there, solid, long after you were gone. The work was hard, but it was real. And in a life that often felt chaotic and uncertain, that realness mattered.*

I am not romanticizing manual labor. I am not suggesting that physical work is inherently nobler or more virtuous than intellectual work, or that poverty builds character, or any of the other patronizing things people sometimes say about hard work when they have never had to do it. What I am saying is that there is dignity in it. A particular kind of dignity that comes from using your body to accomplish something concrete, from mastering a skill that requires not just thought but physical practice, from the knowledge that you are capable of doing things that are genuinely difficult.

And for people who have had that experience - who have worked physically demanding jobs out of necessity - that dignity is real. It does not compensate for the unfairness of needing to work that hard. But it is real, and it is worth naming, because the story of poverty is not only a story of deprivation. It is also, sometimes, a story of competence earned through difficulty.

The Class Divide: When Work Is Seen and When It Is Not

One of the most invisible wounds of class is the way certain kinds of work are socially recognized as valuable, skilled, and worthy of respect - and certain other kinds of work are not. White-collar work is career. Blue-collar work is just a job. Intellectual labor is sophisticated. Manual labor is simple. Office work requires education. Physical work requires only a strong back.

All of these distinctions are false, or at least vastly overstated. But they shape how people are valued, how much they are paid, and how they see themselves. And for people who do physical work - especially when they have the intellectual capacity to do something else but lack the economic resources to access it - the invisibility is felt. The sense that your work does not count in the same way, that your intelligence is not recognized, that the effort you put in is undervalued because the work itself is seen as low-status.

This is not an abstract problem. It shows up in wages, in working conditions, in the basic respect people are afforded or not afforded based on the collar color of their job. And it contributes to something I want to name carefully: the internalized class shame that many working-class people carry, even after they have moved into middle-class professions. The sense that they are not quite legitimate in educated spaces. That they do not belong. That someone will eventually notice and send them back.

8.3 - Education as Battleground: Who Gets to Become Who They Were Meant to Be

Let me tell you something I have thought about a lot over the years. When I was working to pay for college - exhausted, falling asleep in lectures, trying to study on breaks between shifts - there were other students in my biology classes whose biggest concern was whether they wanted to go to medical school or get a PhD. They had the luxury of treating education as a space for exploration, for trying things out, for following intellectual curiosity wherever it led. I did not have that luxury. I was there to get a degree so I could get a job so I could survive. Every credit hour was expensive. Every failed class was a financial disaster.

And the thing I want you to understand is that this difference - this difference in how education is experienced based on whether you are paying for it with money you do not have, or whether it is simply provided as a matter of course - this difference is not just about money. It is about the intellectual freedom to take risks. To fail. To change your mind. To explore.

The Hidden Curriculum: What Education Assumes You Already Know

Education, especially higher education, operates on a set of assumptions that are invisible to the people who grew up with them and glaringly visible to the people who did not. It assumes you know how to talk to professors. How to ask for help. How to navigate bureaucracy. How to manage unstructured time. How to write in the particular style that academic culture values. How to present yourself as someone who belongs in these spaces.

These are not skills you are taught in college. They are skills you are supposed to arrive with. And if you come from a family where no one went to college, where the culture of academia is foreign, where the social and cultural capital that smooths your way through these institutions is simply absent - then you are navigating all of it blind. Figuring it out as you go. Making mistakes that other students do not make because they learned the rules implicitly, through family and social class, long before they ever set foot on a campus.

This is what sociologist Pierre Bourdieu called cultural capital. It is not intelligence. It is not merit. It is familiarity with the codes and norms and unstated expectations of educated spaces. And students who arrive without it are at a disadvantage that is rarely acknowledged, because acknowledging it would require admitting that the playing field is not level. That the meritocracy is not quite as meritocratic as it pretends to be.

> *Education is supposed to be the great equalizer. The pathway from poverty to opportunity. And it can be. But it is a much harder pathway when you have to build the road while walking it - when you are learning the hidden curriculum while working full-time, while sending money home, while carrying the weight of being the first in your family to try.*

When a Parent Withholds Education: The Economics of Control

There is a particular cruelty when a parent who has the means to support their child's education chooses not to. When tuition becomes a tool of control. When financial support is conditional on obedience, or compliance, or the child becoming who the parent wants them to be rather than who they are.

This is not poverty. It is something different - the weaponization of economic power within a family. And it leaves a specific kind of wound: the knowledge that the resources existed, that the support was possible, and that it was withheld. Not because it was not available, but because you were not deemed worthy of it. Or because it could be used to exert power over you. Or because withholding it was a way to punish you for being yourself.

The adult who paid their own way through school when a parent could have helped carries a particular anger. Not the anger of someone who grew up poor and knew their parents were doing their best. That is a different experience, often accompanied by gratitude for the sacrifices parents made. This is the anger of someone who was forced into unnecessary hardship. Who paid a price that should not have been required. Who lost years to exhaustion and financial stress that could have been avoided.

> *I carried that anger for a long time. The sense that I had been made to work harder than I should have, for something that should have been given freely. And the anger was complicated by guilt - because I did make it through, I did get the education, so maybe I had no right to complain. But the anger was real. And it took me years to understand that both things could be true: I succeeded, and I should not have had to fight that hard to do it.*

First-Generation Students and the Invisible Weight

Being the first person in your family to attend college carries its own particular weight. Not just the practical challenges -

the lack of guidance, the cultural unfamiliarity, the financial burden - but the emotional weight of being the one who leaves. Who pursues something the family does not entirely understand. Who succeeds in a world that the family is not part of. And who, in succeeding, sometimes creates distance between themselves and the people they love.

There is a concept called survivor's guilt that is usually applied to people who lived through something that killed others. But there is a version of it that first-generation college students often experience: the guilt of having opportunities that siblings, parents, cousins did not have. The guilt of being the exception. The sense that your success is somehow a betrayal - of your family, of your class, of the place you came from.

This is especially acute when family dynamics are already complicated by trauma. When the education you pursue is also an escape. When staying would have meant remaining in an environment that was harmful, and leaving meant choosing yourself over the people who needed you. The success and the loss are inseparable. You made it out, and the making it out required leaving something behind.

8.4 - The Philosophy of Deserving

Here is a question that lives underneath all of this: do people deserve what they get? Or more precisely: do you deserve what you did not get?

This is not an academic question. It is a question that people who grew up without - without money, without support, without the safety net that others had - live with constantly. It shapes how you see yourself. How you interpret your successes and failures. Whether you believe the opportunities you were denied were something you deserved to have, or whether you internalize the deprivation as evidence of some fundamental unworthiness.

Meritocracy and the Myth of Earned Success

Western capitalist culture loves the idea of meritocracy: that people succeed or fail based on their own merit, their own effort, their own talent. The implication is that success is earned and failure is deserved. If you work hard, you will succeed. If you have not succeeded, you must not have worked hard enough.

This is a comforting narrative for people who have succeeded. It allows them to believe that their success is entirely their own accomplishment, a function of their virtue and effort rather than a function of advantages they happened to inherit. And it is a punishing narrative for people who have failed, or struggled, or worked themselves into the ground without achieving the success they were promised. Because it tells them that their difficulty is their fault. That they did not try hard enough. That they lack what it takes.

The reality, which anyone who looks honestly at the data knows, is that success is the product of both individual effort and structural advantage. Talent matters. Work ethic matters. But so does being born into a family with resources. So does access to good schools. So does not having to work full-time while attending college. So does having a safety net that allows you to take risks without the risk being catastrophic.

The person who succeeded with all of those advantages is not undeserving of their success. But they are also not more deserving than the person who worked just as hard without the advantages and did not succeed, or succeeded only partially, or succeeded at enormous cost. The meritocracy is a myth. And the myth serves the people it advantages while blaming the people it does not.

> *You are not less worthy because you started with less. And the person who started with more is not more worthy because they succeeded with advantages you never had. The game was never fair. And losing an unfair game is not a moral failure.*

Luck, Agency, and the Ethics of Self-Creation

Here is the philosophical tension I have lived with, and that I think many people who have had to build their own lives from scratch live with: you want to believe that your success is your own. That you made yourself. That you earned what you have. Because believing that gives you agency. It says that your life is something you participate in shaping, rather than something that happens to you.

But you also know, if you are honest, that luck played a role. That there were moments when things could have gone differently. That some of the breaks you got were not earned - they were chance. And that some of the hardships you faced were not deserved - they were the result of circumstances you did not choose and could not control.

Philosopher Thomas Nagel has written about what he calls moral luck: the way our moral status - how we judge ourselves and are judged by others - depends on factors beyond our control. You are not responsible for the family you were born into. The country. The era. The genetic lottery. The presence or absence of trauma in your childhood. And yet all of these factors shape who you become and what you are able to accomplish.

This does not mean that effort does not matter. It does. This does not mean that agency is an illusion. It is not. But it does mean that the person you became is the result of a complicated interaction between what you did and what was done to you. Between the choices you made and the choices that were made for you. And holding that complexity - honoring both your agency and your circumstances, both your effort and your luck - is one of the hardest and most important philosophical tasks there is.

What You Owe Yourself - and What You Do Not

One of the lasting wounds of economic adversity, especially when it is compounded by family trauma, is the sense that you owe something. That you have to prove yourself. That you must work harder, achieve more, be more useful, more competent, more indispensable - because that is how you earn the right to exist in spaces where others belong by birthright.

This is exhausting. And it is, ultimately, a lie. You do not owe anyone proof of your worth. You do not have to earn the right to exist. You do not have to be exceptional to deserve care, or rest, or kindness, or the basic resources that make a human life liveable.

But unlearning that belief - the belief that you must earn what others receive freely - is difficult. Because it was learned young, and it was learned in conditions where it was true. Where care was conditional. Where support had to be earned. Where nothing was given freely and everything came with a price.

The philosophical work here is not just intellectual. It is emotional. It is learning to believe, at a level deeper than thought, that you are enough. Not because of what you achieve, but because you are a person. And people, simply by existing, have worth. That is not a claim you have to prove. It is a premise. And it applies to you as much as it applies to anyone.

✦✦✦

I want to close this chapter by speaking directly to anyone who has worked hard for what others were given. Who paid their own way through school. Who sent money home while barely having enough for themselves. Who juggled jobs and classes and exhaustion and still somehow made it through. Who carries the anger of having been forced into unnecessary hardship. Who wonders, sometimes, whether they are allowed to be tired.

You are allowed to be tired. You are allowed to be angry. You are allowed to look at people who had it easier and feel the unfairness of that without being told you are bitter or resentful or that you should just be grateful for what you have.

What you did was hard. It should not have been as hard as it was. And the fact that you succeeded does not mean the hardship was justified or that it built your character or that you should thank the people who made it harder. You succeeded despite the hardship, not because of it. And that is worth acknowledging.

The competence you developed - the ability to work hard, to manage scarcity, to persist through exhaustion, to solve problems without resources - that is real. And it is valuable. But it came at a cost. And you do not have to pretend the cost was worth it. You are allowed to wish it had been different. To wish you had been given what you had to fight for. To wish someone had made it easier.

That does not make you ungrateful. It makes you honest.

Class Is Not Just Money - It Is a Lens Through Which Everything Is Seen

This chapter has moved through difficult territory. The neuro-science of scarcity and how poverty taxes cognitive bandwidth. The dignity of manual labor and the class divide that makes certain work invisible. Education as a battleground, where cultural capital determines who arrives ready to succeed and who has to learn the rules while playing the game. And the philosophy of deserving - the tension between merit and luck, effort and advantage, agency and circumstance.

What ties all of this together is the recognition that class is not just about how much money you have. It is about how you experience the world. Whether you grow up with a safety net or a tightrope. Whether education is an opportunity or a battle. Whether work is a place to develop your potential or a place to exchange your body and time for survival. Whether rest is a luxury you cannot afford or a basic right you take for granted.

And when class intersects with trauma - when you are carrying the wounds of an abusive or neglectful childhood and also navigating economic adversity - the compounding is real. The cognitive bandwidth is taxed from multiple directions at once. The stress is layered. And the path forward is harder than it should be.

But the path forward exists. People who started with nothing have built lives. People who fought for their education have become teachers, scientists, writers, thinkers. People who were told they would not amount to anything have proved that prediction wrong. Not because they were exceptional - though they were strong - but because they refused to accept that their starting point determined their ending point.

If that is you - if you are still building, still fighting, still working harder than you should have to - know this. The world did not make it easy. But you are making it anyway. And that is worth something. It is worth a lot.

⊠ *Part III: The Turn - Chapter 9: What Flourishes in the Dark*

III

The Turn

Resilience, post-traumatic growth, love, consciousness, and the hard, honest, possible work of integration and becoming

9

What Flourishes in the Dark

Resilience, Post-Traumatic Growth, and the Science of Surviving Well

"Resilience is not the absence of being broken. It is the discovery that broken things can still grow."

We have spent eight chapters walking through difficult territory. The architecture of a mind built in chaos. The biology of fear. The attachment wounds. The fragmented self. The depression that moves in and stays. The body that carries what the mind could not hold. The masks worn for survival. The economic wounds that compound everything else.

All of that is true. All of it matters. And none of it is the end of the story.

Because here is the thing about human beings that the deficit model of trauma sometimes misses: we are adaptive. Extraordinarily, almost absurdly adaptive. The same neuroplasticity that allowed childhood adversity to reshape the developing brain is still present, to varying degrees, throughout the lifespan. The brain that learned one way of being can learn another. The nervous system that was calibrated for threat can be recalibrated for safety. The person who survived by becoming many things, or very small, or invisible, can learn - slowly, with difficulty, but genuinely - to be whole.

This is not inspiration. This is not the toxic positivity that tells you trauma made you stronger or that suffering builds character or that everything happens for a reason. I am not interested in any of those narratives. They are insulting to the reality of what trauma costs.

What I am interested in - what the science supports, what lived experience confirms, what this chapter is about - is the simple, complicated, evidence-backed truth that people who have been through terrible things can build good lives. Not despite what happened to them, exactly. And not because of it, as if the suffering were somehow necessary. But through a process of making meaning from it, of finding capacities in themselves they did not know they had, of discovering that the self is more resilient than the trauma tried to convince them it was.

This chapter is the turn. It is where we stop cataloging damage and start examining what is possible. What resilience actually is. What post-traumatic growth means - and what it does not. What the neuroscience of recovery tells us about how people change. And what it means to build a life worth living when the foundation you were given was flawed.

9.1 - What Resilience Actually Is (and Isn't)

The word resilience gets used in a lot of ways, and not all of them are helpful. Sometimes it is used to mean toughness - the ability to endure hardship without complaint, to keep going no matter what, to bounce back quickly from adversity. Sometimes it is used as a way to blame people who are struggling: if they were more resilient, they would be fine. Sometimes it becomes a kind of moral virtue: resilient people are good, admirable, strong. Non-resilient people are weak, broken, deficient.

None of that is what resilience actually means in the scientific literature. So let me be precise.

The Scientific Definition: Positive Adaptation in the Context of Significant Adversity

Resilience, in the research, is defined as the capacity for positive adaptation despite experiencing significant adversity or trauma. That definition has three important components, and each one matters.

First: adversity. Resilience is not about handling everyday stress. It is about responding to genuinely difficult circumstances - poverty, abuse, neglect, loss, trauma. The term only applies when the thing you are dealing with is objectively hard.

Second: positive adaptation. This does not mean being happy all the time or never struggling. It means functioning well enough to maintain relationships, hold down work, take care of basic needs, and continue developing as a person. It means not being destroyed by what happened. That is a low bar in some ways, and an extraordinarily high one in others.

Third: capacity. Resilience is not a fixed trait you either have or do not have. It is a capacity that can be developed, that varies across contexts and time, and that is influenced by both internal factors - temperament, cognitive abilities, coping strategies - and external factors, particularly the presence or absence of supportive relationships.

> *Resilience is not something you are. It is something you do - a set of processes, strategies, and relationships that allow you to adapt to difficulty without being permanently broken by it.*

What Predicts Resilience? The Research

If resilience is a capacity that can be developed, what develops it? What are the factors that make it more likely that someone exposed to trauma will adapt positively rather than being overwhelmed?

The research consistently points to a few key protective factors. None of them guarantees resilience - these are not magic bullets - but statistically, they matter.

The single most robust predictor of resilience is the presence of at least one stable, supportive relationship with an adult. For children, this is often a parent or caregiver, but it does not have to be. A grandparent, a teacher, a mentor, a coach - anyone who provides consistent care, who sees the child, who is reliably present - can serve this function. The relationship does not have to be perfect. It just has to be good enough to provide a secure base.

For adults, the protective factor is similar: social support. People who have friends, family, or therapeutic relationships they can rely on recover from trauma more effectively than people who are isolated. This is not about having a large social network. It is about having even one or two people with whom you can be honest, who will not abandon you when things are difficult, who provide both practical support and emotional validation.

Other predictors include cognitive abilities - particularly the capacity for problem-solving and planning - which allow people to navigate difficult circumstances more effectively. A sense of agency, the belief that your actions matter and can influence outcomes, even if only partially. Emotional regulation skills, the ability to manage strong feelings without being completely overwhelmed by them. And meaning-making: the capacity to construct a coherent narrative about what happened that integrates the trauma into your life story without letting it become the whole story.

None of these are things you either have or do not have. They are all skills that can be learned, capacities that can be developed, relationships that can be built. That is the hopeful part. Resilience is not a lottery you either won or lost. It is a process you can participate in.

What Resilience Is Not

Let me be very clear about what resilience does not mean, because there are misunderstandings about this that do real harm.

Resilience does not mean you were not hurt. It does not mean the trauma was not that bad, or that you are fine, or that you do not need help. It does not mean you should be over it by now. It does not mean you are not allowed to struggle, or to have bad days, or to need support. It does not mean you have to be strong all the time, or that asking for help is weakness, or that needing therapy means you failed at resilience.

Resilience is not the absence of pain. It is the presence of the capacity to keep going despite the pain. To function despite the struggle. To build a life even when building feels impossibly hard. It is not thriving. It is often just surviving, but surviving in a way that leaves room for something more than survival.

And here is the most important thing: resilience is not your responsibility to prove. You do not owe anyone resilience. The fact that you made it this far - that you are alive, that you are reading this, that you got through whatever you got through - is already evidence of resilience. Whether or not you are thriving. Whether or not you are happy. Whether or not you look, from the outside, like you have it together.

You survived. That is resilience. Everything beyond survival is not a requirement. It is a possibility.

9.2 - Post-Traumatic Growth: When Suffering Changes the Coordinates

In the mid-1990s, psychologists Richard Tedeschi and Lawrence Calhoun began studying something that had been observed anecdotally for a long time but had not been rigorously researched: the phenomenon of people who, after experiencing significant trauma, reported not just recovery but growth. Not just returning to baseline, but changing in ways they described as positive. Becoming, in some fundamental sense, different people than they would have been if the trauma had not occurred.

They called this post-traumatic growth, and they were careful to distinguish it from resilience. Resilience is about maintaining function despite adversity. Post-traumatic growth is about transformation. About the trauma changing not just your circumstances but your priorities, your values, your sense of what matters, your understanding of yourself and the world.

The Five Domains of Post-Traumatic Growth

Tedeschi and Calhoun identified five areas in which people commonly report growth following trauma:

First: greater appreciation of life. A heightened awareness of the preciousness and fragility of existence. The sense that ordinary moments - a conversation with a friend, a meal, the feeling of sun on your skin - matter more than they used to. That life, for all its difficulty, is worth paying attention to.

Second: warmer, more intimate relationships with others. Many people who survive trauma report that their relationships deepen. They become more selective about who they spend time with, but more genuine with the people they choose. They have less patience for superficiality and more capacity for real connection. The mask comes off, slowly, and what emerges is a person capable of intimacy in ways they were not before.

Third: a greater sense of personal strength. Not the belief that they are invulnerable - quite the opposite. But the knowledge, earned through experience, that they can survive things they did not think they could survive. That they are capable of enduring, of adapting, of continuing to exist even when existence is difficult. This is not arrogance. It is a kind of quiet confidence born from having been tested.

Fourth: recognition of new possibilities. Trauma often closes doors. It limits options, constrains futures, forecloses paths that seemed available before. But it also, paradoxically, opens doors that would not have been visible otherwise. People report discovering interests, careers, relationships, ways of being that they would never have encountered if their life had gone according to the original plan. The detour becomes the path.

Fifth: spiritual or existential change. This does not necessarily mean religious conversion, though for some people it does. More often it means a shift in what feels meaningful. A reordering of priorities. The recognition that the things you thought mattered - status, achievement, wealth, appearance - matter less than you believed, and that other things - connection, authenticity, compassion, the quality of your inner life - matter more.

> *Post-traumatic growth is not the claim that trauma is good or necessary. It is the observation that some people, having been through terrible things, become different in ways they value - not because the suffering was worth it, but because they made something from it that the suffering itself did not intend.*

Growth and Suffering Coexist

Here is the part that is crucial to understand: post-traumatic growth does not mean you are healed. It does not mean the trauma is over or that you are no longer affected by it. It is entirely possible - in fact, it is common - to experience both ongoing struggle and genuine growth at the same time.

You can have PTSD and also have a deeper appreciation for life. You can struggle with depression and also have relationships that are more meaningful than they were before. You can carry chronic pain and also have a sense of personal strength you did not have. Growth does not erase suffering. It exists alongside it.

This is important because there is a cultural narrative that says if you have grown from trauma, you should be grateful for it. That you should thank the experience. That the growth justifies the suffering. And that narrative is both wrong and harmful.

The growth is real. And the cost was too high. Both of those things are true. You can value what you learned about yourself and still wish you had learned it a different way. You can be proud of your strength and still be angry that you had to develop it. You can have built a meaningful life from the ruins and still grieve what was destroyed.

Post-traumatic growth is not gratitude for the trauma. It is the human capacity to make meaning from suffering - which is not the same as saying the suffering was meaningful.

> *Research note: Studies show that post-traumatic growth is most likely to occur when certain conditions are met: when the trauma is severe enough to challenge core beliefs, when there is time and space for reflection, when social support is available, and when the person actively engages in meaning-making rather than avoidance. Growth is not automatic. It is a process that requires both internal work and external support.*

9.3 - The Neuroscience of Recovery: Neuroplasticity as Hope

Everything we have discussed so far in this book about what trauma does to the brain - the altered stress response, the hyperactive amygdala, the reduced hippocampal volume, the prefrontal cortex that goes offline under stress - all of that is grounded in a principle we have mentioned repeatedly but have not yet examined in detail: neuroplasticity.

Neuroplasticity is the brain's capacity to change its structure and function in response to experience. It is the mechanism by which we learn anything - language, skills, habits, fears. It is also the mechanism by which we can unlearn, relearn, and change patterns that no longer serve us.

And it is the biological foundation of every claim in this chapter about resilience, growth, and recovery. Without neuroplasticity, none of it would be possible. The brain would be fixed by early experience, and change would be an illusion. But neuroplasticity is real. And it persists, to varying degrees, throughout thc human lifespan.

How the Brain Changes: The Mechanisms

Neuroplasticity happens through several related processes, and understanding them helps demystify what recovery actually requires.

The first is synaptic plasticity: the strengthening or weakening of connections between neurons based on how often they fire together. This is Hebb's Law - neurons that fire together, wire together. And the inverse is also true: neurons that stop firing together weaken their connections. This is the mechanism by which new habits form and old habits fade. It is why practice matters. It is why repetition, consistency, and time are necessary for change.

The second is neurogenesis: the growth of new neurons, particularly in the hippocampus. For many years, neuroscience believed that neurogenesis stopped in childhood. We now know that is false. The adult hippocampus continues to generate new neurons throughout life, and this process is enhanced by certain experiences - exercise, learning, enriched environments - and suppressed by others, particularly chronic stress and depression. The hippocampus that was damaged by prolonged cortisol exposure can, under the right conditions, begin to repair itself. This is not metaphorical healing. It is literal regrowth.

The third is changes in connectivity: the formation of new neural pathways and the pruning of old ones. The brain is not a static circuit board. It is a dynamic network that reorganizes itself based on what it does. When you repeatedly practice a new skill - whether that skill is emotional regulation, or social engagement, or simply pausing before reacting - you are not just learning something. You are changing the physical structure of your brain. Building new connections. Making the new pattern easier to access and the old pattern harder to fall into.

> The *brain that was shaped by trauma can be reshaped by recovery. Not erased. Not returned to some imagined pre-trauma state. But genuinely changed, in ways that make the future different from the past.*

What Supports Neuroplasticity: The Conditions for Change

Neuroplasticity does not happen automatically. It requires certain conditions. And understanding those conditions is important, because it tells us what actually supports recovery.

Safety is foundational. The nervous system that is in chronic threat mode is not in learning mode. The brain under stress prioritizes survival over growth. For neuroplasticity to occur - for new patterns to form, for the hippocampus to generate new neurons, for the prefrontal cortex to strengthen its regulatory capacity - the nervous system needs to feel safe enough to stand down from high alert. This is why therapeutic environments emphasize safety first. Not because safety is the end goal, but because it is the precondition for everything else.

Repetition and consistency matter enormously. One good therapy session does not rewire the brain. One moment of feeling calm does not undo years of hypervigilance. Change happens through accumulation. Through repeated experiences that slowly, incrementally, teach the nervous system a new pattern.

This is frustrating, because it is slow. But it is also reassuring, because it means that small, consistent efforts compound over time.

Novelty and challenge are also important. The brain changes most when it is learning something new, when it is challenged in ways that require adaptation. This is why therapy that simply rehashes the past without introducing new ways of thinking or relating is often less effective than therapy that actively teaches new skills. The brain needs something to work with. Something to practice. Something that is different enough from the old pattern that new neural pathways have to form.

And finally: relationships. Co-regulation, which we discussed in Chapter 6 in the context of polyvagal theory, is one of the most powerful tools for promoting neuroplasticity. When your nervous system is in the presence of another nervous system that is calm, regulated, and safe, your nervous system begins to entrain to that pattern. Over time, through repeated experiences of co-regulation, the brain learns what safety feels like in the body. And that felt sense of safety is what allows deeper change to occur.

The Limits of Neuroplasticity: What We Can and Cannot Change

I want to be honest about the limits, because false hope is not useful and because the truth is more respectful.

Neuroplasticity decreases with age. The young brain is more plastic than the adult brain. This does not mean adults cannot change - they can, and they do - but it does mean change is slower and requires more effort. The patterns laid down in childhood are particularly durable, not because they are permanent, but because they were formed during a period of maximal plasticity and have been reinforced for decades. Changing them is possible. But it is not quick.

Some changes are easier than others. Learning a new skill, forming a new habit, developing a new way of thinking - these are within the range of what neuroplasticity readily supports. Completely erasing trauma memories, eliminating all symptoms of PTSD, or returning to a hypothetical pre-trauma baseline - these are not realistic goals. The brain that went through trauma will always have gone through trauma. The memory exists. The history exists. What changes is your relationship to it. Your capacity to live with it without being controlled by it.

And some people, despite their best efforts and the best available interventions, continue to struggle. Neuroplasticity is real, but it is not magic. Not everyone recovers fully. Not everyone experiences post-traumatic growth. And that is not a failure of effort or character or willingness to heal. It is the reality that trauma is powerful, that brains are complex, and that outcomes are not entirely within individual control.

But the possibility of change is real. And for many people, that possibility is enough to keep trying.

9.4 - Meaning-Making: Viktor Frankl, the Stoics, and the Philosophical Necessity of Narrative

There is a dimension of resilience and growth that is not purely biological or psychological. It is philosophical. It is the question of meaning. What does it mean that this happened to you? How do you integrate the experience into a coherent sense of who you are? How do you make a life that is not defined entirely by what was done to you, but that also does not pretend it never happened?

This is the work of meaning-making. And it is, I would argue, one of the most important and most difficult tasks of recovery.

Viktor Frankl and the Search for Meaning

Viktor Frankl was an Austrian psychiatrist who survived Auschwitz. His wife, his parents, and most of his family did not. What he brought out of that experience - in addition to his life - was a theory about what makes human suffering bearable. He called it logotherapy, and its central claim is this: human beings can endure almost any suffering if they can find meaning in it.

Frankl did not mean that suffering is inherently meaningful. Auschwitz was not meaningful. It was evil, senseless, a horror that should never have happened. But Frankl observed that among the prisoners, those who survived tended to be those who had found some purpose, some reason to continue. A loved one they wanted to see again. A task they wanted to complete. A future they were determined to reach. The meaning was not in the suffering. It was in what they chose to do with it.

He wrote: 'When we are no longer able to change a situation, we are challenged to change ourselves.' This is not resignation. It is the recognition that while we cannot always control what happens to us, we can control how we interpret it, how we respond to it, and what we make of it going forward.

For trauma survivors, this means that the question is not 'why did this happen to me?' - a question that often has no satisfying answer. The question is 'what do I do now that it has happened?' That is a question with many possible answers. And finding one that feels true, that gives direction, that provides a reason to continue - that is meaning-making.

> *Meaning is not found in the trauma. It is made from the trauma - constructed deliberately, over time, through the choices you make about what the experience will mean for the person you become.*

The Stoics: What Is and Is Not Within Your Control

The ancient Stoic philosophers - Epictetus, Marcus Aurelius, Seneca - were obsessed with a distinction that is central to psychological resilience: the difference between what is within your control and what is not.

Epictetus, who was born a slave and later became a philosopher, taught that most of what happens to us is not within our control. We do not control other people's actions. We do not control the circumstances of our birth, the accidents that befall us, the illnesses that strike, the losses we suffer. All of that is external. All of that is beyond the reach of our will.

What is within our control, Epictetus said, is how we respond. Our judgments. Our interpretations. Our values. Our choices about what to do next. No one can take those from you, no matter what they do to you. Even in the worst circumstances, even when all external freedom is gone, the freedom to choose your response remains.

This is not a claim that response is easy. It is not minimizing the power of circumstance or trauma. It is a claim about where agency lives. And for people who have had so much taken from them - who were children without power, who were harmed by people they could not escape - the Stoic distinction offers something valuable: the recognition that even if you could not control what was done to you, you can control what you do with it now.

The past is not within your control. It happened. But the future is not yet written. And the story you tell about the past - the meaning you make from it - is something you participate in creating.

Narrative and the Construction of a Coherent Self

Human beings are storytelling creatures. We do not experience our lives as a series of disconnected moments. We experience them as a narrative. A story with a beginning, a middle, and - eventually - an ending. And the way we tell that story to ourselves shapes who we believe we are.

Trauma disrupts narrative. It creates gaps, silences, fragments that do not fit into a coherent story. The person you were before the trauma and the person you became after can feel like different people. And the work of recovery is, in part, the work of creating a narrative that holds both. That integrates the trauma into the larger story of your life without letting it become the entire story.

This is not about positive thinking. It is not about reframing trauma as a gift or a lesson or something you should be grateful for. It is about constructing a narrative that is true - that acknowledges what happened, what it cost, and also what you have done with it. The resilience you have shown. The growth you have experienced. The person you are becoming, not despite the trauma but in the ongoing process of living with it and beyond it.

Therapies like narrative therapy work explicitly with this process: helping people reauthor their stories in ways that give them agency, that recognize their strengths, that refuse to let trauma be the only thing that defines them. The story does not change the facts. But it changes the meaning. And meaning, as Frankl knew, is what makes suffering bearable.

✦✦✦

Let me close this chapter by saying something directly.

If you have read this far - through eight chapters of what trauma does, what it costs, how it shapes the brain and the body and the self - and you are still here, still reading, still asking whether change is possible, then you already know something important about yourself.

You are resilient. Not because you never struggle. Not because you are fine. But because you are still here. Still engaged. Still asking the questions. Still, in whatever way you can manage, moving forward.

That is not a small thing. That is the foundation. Everything else - the growth, the healing, the meaning-making - builds on that foundation. You are already doing the hardest part, which is continuing to exist in a body and a mind that were shaped by difficulty. The rest is not easy. But it is possible. And you are already proving that you are capable of doing difficult things.

The Turn Has Begun - and the Path Forward Is Real

This chapter marks the shift from diagnosis to possibility. From cataloging damage to examining what can be built. We have looked at what resilience actually is - not a fixed trait, but a process, a capacity that develops through relationships and practice and the accumulation of experiences that prove you can survive difficult things.

We have explored post-traumatic growth - the genuine, documented phenomenon of people who become different, in ways they value, through the process of surviving and making meaning from trauma. Not because the trauma was good, but because they made something from it that the trauma did not intend.

We have walked through the neuroscience of recovery and the reality of neuroplasticity - the brain's capacity to change, to form new patterns, to heal in ways that are measurable and real. Not quick. Not complete. But genuine.

And we have examined meaning-making - the philosophical work of constructing a narrative that holds both what happened and who you are becoming. The Stoic wisdom of focusing on what is within your control. Frankl's insistence that meaning can be made even from the worst suffering. The narrative work of integrating trauma into a larger story without letting it be the whole story.

What comes next - in the final three chapters - is the practical dimension of all this theory. How to love when you never learned how. What consciousness and suffering tell us about the nature of self. And finally, the long work of integration, of building a life in the ruins, of becoming - slowly, imperfectly, genuinely - whole.

The turn has begun. The path forward is real. And you are already walking it.

10

Loving Without a Map

Adult Relationships When the Template Was Never Written

"To love without a model is to navigate by stars you have to name yourself."

Here is a question that lives underneath almost every relationship difficulty for people who grew up without secure attachment: how do you love someone when you were never shown what love looks like?

Not love as an abstract concept. Not the cultural scripts about romance and partnership that saturate our media. But love as a lived, embodied practice - the day-to-day reality of being close to someone, trusting someone, needing someone, letting yourself be needed in return. How do you do that when your earliest experiences of closeness were chaotic, or conditional, or absent altogether?

This chapter is about adult relationships when the internal working model - the template we discussed in Chapter 3 - was built from scarcity, unpredictability, or harm. It is about what happens when you want connection but do not quite trust it. When you need intimacy but find it terrifying. When you are drawn to people who feel familiar in ways that are not good for you, or when you push away people who are actually safe because safety itself feels wrong.

And it is about something that the research on attachment increasingly supports and that many people discover through painful experience: that the patterns you learned in childhood are not permanent. That attachment styles can change. That you can learn, as an adult, what you were never taught as a child. That love can be learned.

It is not easy. It is not quick. But it is possible. And this chapter is about how.

10.1 - Repetition Compulsion: Why We Recreate What Hurt Us

One of the strangest and most frustrating patterns that trauma survivors recognize in themselves is this: they keep ending up in relationships that hurt them in familiar ways. Not identical to the original wound, but similar enough that the pain has a recognizable shape. The person who grew up with an unpredictable parent finds themselves drawn to unpredictable partners. The person who was neglected finds themselves with people who are emotionally unavailable. The person who learned that love came with violence ends up in relationships where conflict escalates in ways that feel dangerous.

Why? Why would anyone choose - and it does not feel like a choice, but that is what makes it so confusing - to recreate the conditions that hurt them?

Freud's Repetition Compulsion: The Unconscious Drive to Resolve

Sigmund Freud, for all the ways his theories have been revised or discarded, identified something that has survived decades of more rigorous research: the repetition compulsion. The unconscious tendency to recreate traumatic situations in an attempt to master them. To get it right this time. To have a different ending.

The logic, to the extent that the unconscious has logic, is this: if I can find someone who resembles the person who hurt me, and if I can make them love me, then I will have finally succeeded. I will have proved that I am lovable. That the original rejection or harm was not about me. That I can win the game I lost as a child.

This is, of course, doomed. Because the person you are trying to fix is not the person who hurt you. They are just someone who resembles them. And even if you succeed in getting them to love you - which is unlikely, because people who are unavailable or harmful tend to remain so - it does not heal the original wound. It does not go back and fix what happened. The child who needed love does not get it retroactively just because the adult version of you managed to extract it from someone who was not inclined to give it.

But the pattern persists because it is unconscious. It operates below the level of deliberate choice. You do not wake up one day and decide to pursue someone who will hurt you in familiar ways. You just feel drawn to them. They feel right. Interesting. Alive. The person who is actually safe, who is emotionally available and kind and consistent - that person feels boring. Or wrong. Or somehow suspicious, as if their goodness is a performance that will eventually reveal itself as a lie.

> *Familiar feels like home, even when home was not a good place. The nervous system mistakes familiarity for safety, and so you keep walking back into rooms that hurt you, hoping this time the ending will be different.*

The Neuroscience of Attraction to the Familiar

There is a neurological dimension to this that is worth understanding. The brain's reward system - the dopamine pathways that signal wanting, craving, motivation - is activated most strongly not by things that are reliably good, but by things that are unpredictably good. This is why gambling is addictive. This is why intermittent reinforcement is more powerful than consistent reinforcement. The uncertainty creates a kind of neurochemical suspense that the brain finds compelling.

A relationship with someone who is consistently kind and available does not activate this system in the same way. It is good, yes. But it is predictable. The brain, which was trained in an environment where love was scarce and unpredictable, does not register predictable goodness as exciting. It registers it as flat. The dopamine does not surge. The feeling of aliveness that comes with uncertainty - will they text back, will they be warm or cold tonight, will I finally be enough - is absent.

And so the person who is actually good for you feels wrong. Not because they are wrong, but because your nervous system was trained to associate love with uncertainty. With working for it. With the high of finally getting it and the crash of losing it again. That pattern is terrible for long-term wellbeing. But it is deeply, neurologically compelling.

Breaking this pattern requires recognizing it. Seeing clearly that the pull you feel toward someone is not evidence that they are right for you. It is evidence that they are familiar. And familiarity, when your childhood was difficult, is not a reliable guide. You have to learn to tolerate the discomfort of what feels unfamiliar - steadiness, reliability, boring goodness - long enough for your nervous system to recalibrate. To learn that safe can also be home.

The Partner as Parent: Transference in Adult Relationships

There is a concept from psychoanalysis that describes something many people experience but rarely name: transference. The process by which feelings and patterns from past relationships - particularly early relationships with caregivers - get transferred onto new relationships, particularly romantic ones.

In practice, this looks like treating your partner as if they were your parent. Not consciously. Not deliberately. But unconsciously expecting them to meet needs that were never met in childhood. Or reacting to them as if they were the person who hurt you, even when they are not. Or testing them, over and over, to see if they will abandon you the way you were abandoned, so that you can finally prove to yourself that everyone leaves.

This puts an enormous burden on a partner who did not sign up to be your parent. Who is trying to be an equal adult in an adult relationship, but keeps getting cast in a role they do not understand and cannot fill. And it creates dynamics that are toxic: the constant need for reassurance that can never be satisfied, the hair-trigger reactions to perceived slights, the inability to trust that someone can love you and also need space, or disagree with you and still be committed.

The work here - and it is hard work, often requiring therapy to do well - is to recognize when you are relating to your partner as if they were someone else. To catch yourself in the act of transference and pause. To ask: is this actually about them, or is this an old wound being triggered? And then to communicate that distinction. To say, out loud: I know you are not my parent. I know you are not trying to hurt me. But something you did reminded me of something old, and I need a moment to separate the past from the present.

That level of self-awareness is difficult. But it is also one of the most powerful tools for breaking repetition patterns. Because once you can see the pattern, you can choose differently. The unconscious becomes conscious. And consciousness, slow as it is, gives you back some measure of control.

10.2 - Vulnerability and the Armored Heart

Intimacy requires vulnerability. This is not a poetic claim. It is a definitional one. To be intimate with someone means to let them see you - not the performed version, not the mask, but the actual you, with all the mess and uncertainty and need that entails. And for people whose early experiences taught them that vulnerability is dangerous, this is one of the hardest asks there is.

Why the Armor Went On in the First Place

The armor - the emotional walls, the self-sufficiency that refuses help, the performance of not needing anyone - did not develop because you are cold or unfeeling. It developed because you needed it. Because in the environment where it was built, vulnerability invited harm. Showing need meant being dismissed, or mocked, or hurt. Asking for help meant being told you were too much, too needy, too weak. So you learned to need nothing. Or to need quietly, invisibly, in ways that would not cost you.

The armor worked. It kept you safe. It got you through a childhood where safety required self-sufficiency. And it followed you into adulthood, where it keeps operating long after the original danger has passed.

The problem is that the armor that protects you from harm also protects you from connection. The walls that keep out the people who might hurt you also keep out the people who might love you. And the longer the armor stays on, the more it feels like part of you - like removing it would leave you exposed, raw, defenseless in a world that still feels dangerous.

> *The armored heart is not a cold heart. It is a heart that learned, rightly, that openness was dangerous. And it is still waiting for evidence that the world has changed enough to make openness safe.*

The Catch-22: You Cannot Be Loved Without Being Seen

Here is the impossibility at the center of intimacy for trauma survivors: you want to be loved. Deeply. You are not incapable of love or averse to it. But love requires being known. And being known requires letting someone see you. And letting someone see you feels like handing them a weapon.

So you find yourself in relationships where you are close but not too close. Where you share some things but keep the hardest things private. Where you are present but guarded. And your partner senses this. They feel the wall. They know there is more of you that you are not showing. And either they respect it and maintain the distance, in which case the relationship stays safe but shallow. Or they push, trying to get closer, and you push back, because pushing feels like invasion.

This is not sustainable. A relationship cannot deepen if one person is perpetually armored. But removing the armor feels impossible, because the fear underneath it is real. The belief that if someone saw all of you - the trauma, the damage, the ways you are still struggling - they would leave. That the real you is not lovable. That the armor is not hiding something valuable. It is hiding something broken.

The work of learning to be vulnerable is the work of testing that belief. Slowly. With someone who has earned the right to see you. Not all at once - that would be overwhelming for both of you. But incrementally. Letting someone see a little more. Sharing something you usually keep private. Asking for help with something you would normally handle alone. And then, crucially, seeing what happens.

Most of the time, if you have chosen well, nothing terrible happens. They do not leave. They do not mock you. They do not use the information against you. They just... see you. And they stay. And that experience - repeated enough times, with enough consistency - begins to teach your nervous system something new. That vulnerability, in the right context, with the right person, is not the prelude to harm. It is the prelude to being known. And being known, it turns out, is what love actually is.

Learning to Need: The Hardest Vulnerability

For many trauma survivors, the hardest form of vulnerability is not showing pain or admitting fear. It is needing. Asking for something. Expressing a want and waiting, exposed, to see if it will be met.

Because needing someone gives them power over you. If you do not need them, they cannot hurt you by withholding. But if you let yourself need them - let yourself depend on them for comfort, or support, or presence - then you are at their mercy. And if your early experiences taught you that mercy was in short supply, this feels like unacceptable risk.

So you become self-sufficient. Aggressively so. You handle everything yourself. You do not ask for help. You pride yourself on not needing anyone. And on the surface, this looks like strength. But underneath, it is loneliness. The exhaustion of carrying everything alone. The quiet resentment that no one is helping, even though you never asked and would refuse if they offered.

Learning to need someone is learning to trust that they will show up. Not perfectly. Not every time. But enough times, with enough consistency, that the risk of needing them feels worth it. This does not happen quickly. It does not happen just by deciding to trust. It happens through experience. Through asking for something small and having it be met. And then asking for something slightly larger. And then larger still. Building, over time, a body of evidence that contradicts the old model. That says: this person is different. This relationship is different. Needing is not the same dangerous thing it used to be.

10.3 - Queer Love and the Compounded Closet

For those who are both trauma survivors and queer - carrying the wounds of childhood adversity and the experience of navigating a world that does not fully accept or understand your identity - the challenge of adult relationships is compounded in specific ways that deserve to be named.

Because you are not just learning to love without a map. You are learning to love in a way that the dominant culture did not model for you. In a way that your family may not have accepted. In a way that, for much of your life, you may have had to hide.

The Double Concealment: Trauma and Identity

We talked in Chapter 7 about the exhaustion of carrying multiple concealments. Of hiding the trauma and hiding your identity simultaneously. And nowhere is this compounding more acute than in relationships. Because romantic relationships are where both the trauma history and the queer identity become most visible. Most undeniable. Most in need of integration.

When you enter a relationship as a queer person with a trauma history, you are navigating layers that most people do not have to consciously think about. You are managing your own attachment wounds - the ways you learned to mistrust closeness, to armor yourself, to perform rather than be. And you are also managing the question of visibility. Of whether this relationship can be public. Of whether your family will accept it. Of whether the world will see you as you are or force you back into hiding.

And these two forms of woundedness interact. The trauma made vulnerability difficult. And the closet made authenticity dangerous. So you enter relationships carrying both: the fear of being seen as wounded, and the fear of being seen as queer. And the question becomes: can you let someone see both? Can you trust them with the full truth of who you are - not just the fact of your queerness, but the complexity of your history? Or do you partition yourself, showing them the identity but hiding the wound, or showing them the wound but hiding the self?

> *Queer love after trauma is the radical act of being seen in all your complexity - wounded and whole, hidden and revealed, still becoming who you are - and trusting that you will not be abandoned for it.*

The Absence of Models: Learning a Love You Never Saw

One of the specific challenges of queer relationships is the absence of models. Most people, growing up, see hundreds of examples of what heterosexual relationships look like. In their families, in their communities, in every movie and TV show and book. They absorb, without consciously learning, the scripts and norms and patterns of how those relationships work.

Queer people do not get that. Or they get much less of it. Depending on when and where you grew up, you may have seen very few - or zero - examples of healthy same-sex relationships. No models for what queer partnership looks like. No inherited wisdom about how to navigate conflict, or define roles, or build a life together when the cultural scripts do not apply.

This means that queer relationships require more conscious negotiation. More deliberate communication. More figuring out, together, what this relationship is and how it works, because you cannot just default to the cultural template. This can be exhausting. But it also creates an opportunity: the chance to build something that is genuinely yours. Not inherited. Not performed. Constructed from the ground up, by two people who are choosing, together, what love will look like for them.

And for trauma survivors, who already have to do the work of learning to love without a secure attachment model, this doubling of the challenge can be overwhelming. You are learning to trust when trust was never safe. And you are learning to build a relationship in a form that the world did not teach you. Both at once. It is a lot.

But it is also, in a strange way, liberating. Because when there is no script to follow, you get to write your own. The absence of a map means you have to navigate by feel, by conversation, by trial and error. And that is hard. But it also means that the relationship you build is not constrained by someone else's expectations of what it should be. It can be exactly what you and your partner decide it will be. Nothing more. Nothing less.

Chosen Family and the Relationships That Heal

One of the most important concepts in queer community is chosen family: the people who are not related to you by blood but who function as family. Who show up. Who care. Who see you and do not turn away.

For many queer people, especially those whose families of origin did not accept them, chosen family becomes the primary site of love and support. And for trauma survivors, chosen family can be the place where secure attachment is finally, belatedly, formed. Where you learn what it feels like to be reliably cared for. To have people who know your history and stay. To be part of something that feels like belonging.

This is not a replacement for romantic partnership. But it is often a necessary foundation. Because learning to trust in a romantic relationship is easier when you have already experienced trustworthy relationships elsewhere. When you have friends who have proved, over time, that they will not abandon you. That you can be yourself with them. That your queerness and your trauma history are not deal-breakers but just parts of who you are.

Chosen family is where many queer trauma survivors learn, for the first time, what secure attachment feels like. And that learning becomes the foundation for everything else. For the romantic relationships that come after. For the capacity to let someone in. For the belief - fragile at first, but growing stronger with evidence - that you are lovable, exactly as you are.

10.4 - Earned Secure Attachment: Love Can Be Learned

Everything I have described so far in this chapter - the repetition compulsion, the armored heart, the difficulty of vulnerability, the specific challenges of queer love after trauma - all of it points toward a single question: is change possible? Can the attachment style you developed in childhood be modified in adulthood? Can you learn, as an adult, what you were never taught as a child?

The answer, backed by decades of research, is yes. Not easily. Not quickly. But genuinely, yes.

The Research on Earned Security

In the 1980s and 1990s, as attachment research matured, researchers began studying adults and asking a crucial question: are attachment styles stable across the lifespan, or can they change? The answer turned out to be complicated. For many people, attachment style is relatively stable. The person who had secure attachment in childhood tends to have secure attachment in adulthood. The person who had insecure attachment tends to carry that forward.

But not always. A significant minority of adults who had insecure attachment in childhood show patterns of secure attachment in adulthood. Researchers called this earned secure attachment. And the finding was important not just because it showed that change was possible, but because it revealed what makes change possible.

People who achieved earned security had done one or more of the following: engaged in significant therapy, particularly therapy that focused on understanding and processing their attachment history; formed a long-term relationship with a partner who had secure attachment and who provided a consistent, reliable, emotionally available presence; or engaged in deep self-reflection and meaning-making, often through journaling, spiritual practice, or other forms of intentional introspection.

What all of these pathways have in common is time and repetition. Earned security is not a sudden insight or a single corrective experience. It is the accumulation of thousands of small moments that contradict the old internal working model. That teach the nervous system, slowly and through direct experience, that closeness can be safe. That people can be reliable. That you are worthy of love.

> *You can learn, as an adult, what you were never taught as a child. Attachment styles are not fixed. The map you were given can be redrawn. It is slow work, and it*

> *requires the right conditions - but it is real.*

What a Secure Partner Provides

One of the most powerful pathways to earned security is a relationship with a securely attached partner. Not because they fix you - relationships do not work that way - but because they provide, consistently and over time, the experience of secure attachment that you did not have in childhood.

What does a securely attached partner actually do? They show up. They are emotionally available. They respond to bids for connection rather than dismissing them. They can tolerate conflict without it becoming a threat to the relationship. They are comfortable with both closeness and independence. They do not punish you for having needs. They do not require you to perform or earn their love.

More specifically: when you are anxious, they reassure you without making you feel like a burden. When you pull away, they give you space but do not disappear. When you are struggling, they offer support without trying to fix you. When you make mistakes, they stay. When you are vulnerable, they respond with care rather than judgment.

This is not a personality type. It is a skill set. And crucially, it is something that can be learned. A person who grew up with secure attachment may naturally have these skills. But a person who did not can develop them through therapy, through self-work, and through the deliberate practice of showing up for a partner in these ways.

What this means is that even if both partners come to the relationship with insecure attachment - and this is common, because people tend to be drawn to others with similar attachment histories - both can work toward greater security together. It is not ideal. It is harder when neither person starts from a secure base. But it is possible. Two people can learn, together, to be the secure base for each other that neither of them had.

Therapy as Attachment Repair

The other major pathway to earned security is therapy. Not all therapy, and not every therapeutic relationship - but therapy that specifically addresses attachment, that provides a safe and consistent relationship over time, and that allows the client to experience something they may never have experienced: being truly seen, accepted, and reliably cared for by someone who is present week after week, who does not abandon them when things get difficult, who can tolerate their anger and fear and shame without retaliating or withdrawing.

This is, fundamentally, what the therapeutic relationship does when it works: it provides a corrective emotional experience. It gives you a chance to form a secure attachment with your therapist - to learn, in that relationship, what secure attachment feels like - and then to generalize that learning to other relationships.

It takes time. Often years. And it requires finding a therapist who is skilled, who understands attachment, and who is capable of providing the kind of steady, attuned presence that secure attachment requires. But when it works, the change is real. People report that their relationships outside therapy begin to shift. That they are more comfortable with closeness, more able to trust, less reactive to perceived threats, more capable of asking for what they need and receiving it.

Therapy does not give you back the childhood you should have had. Nothing can do that. But it can give you, now, the relationship you needed then. And that relationship, internalized over time, becomes a new model. A new map. One that says: closeness is possible. Safety is possible. You are lovable. Not because you have proved it through achievement or performance, but simply because you are.

✦✦✦

Let me close this chapter by speaking directly to anyone who is navigating relationships while carrying attachment wounds.

Love is harder for you than it is for people who grew up secure. That is not a moral failing. It is not evidence that you are broken. It is the predictable outcome of learning about relationships in conditions that were not safe. The patterns you developed - the armor, the vigilance, the difficulty trusting, the way you push people away or cling too hard - those made sense. They kept you safe when safety was scarce.

But they do not have to be permanent. The research on earned security tells us that the brain can learn new patterns. That the nervous system can be retrained. That you can develop, as an adult, the secure attachment that childhood did not give you. It is not easy. It requires the right partner or the right therapist, and often both. It requires time and patience and a willingness to be uncomfortable while your nervous system learns to trust something new.

But it is possible. People do it. Not everyone, and not all at once, but enough people that we know the pathway exists. You can learn to love in ways that feel safe. You can learn to let someone see you without the armor. You can learn that needing someone is not the prelude to being hurt.

The map you were given was incomplete. But you can draw a new one. Line by line, experience by experience, relationship by relationship. It is slow work. But it is some of the most important work there is.

Love Is Not Beyond You - It Just Requires a Different Kind of Learning

This chapter has walked through some of the hardest territory in the book: how to build intimate relationships when the foundation for intimacy was never properly laid. We have examined repetition compulsion and why familiar feels safe even when familiar hurt you. The armored heart and why vulnerability feels impossible when openness was once dangerous. The specific challenges of queer love when identity and trauma compound. And the science of earned secure attachment - the evidence that love can, genuinely, be learned.

What I want you to take from this is not that relationships will be easy if you just do the work. They will not. Relationships are difficult for everyone, and they are more difficult when you are starting from insecure attachment. The learning curve is steeper. The mistakes are more costly. The fear is more present.

But difficulty is not impossibility. And the fact that you have to learn something others were given does not mean you are incapable of learning it. It just means you are learning it later, with less support, and from a harder starting point. And that is worth acknowledging. Not as an excuse, but as context. As recognition of what you are actually doing when you try to love someone after everything you have been through.

You are rewriting a script that was written in conditions you did not choose. You are building skills that others developed passively through secure childhoods. You are trusting when trust was never safe, needing when need was punished, and letting yourself be seen when visibility once meant danger.

That is not easy. But you are doing it. And every time you choose to try again, to stay present in discomfort, to let someone a little closer despite the fear - you are proving that earned security is not just a research finding. It is a lived reality. And it is available to you.

⊠ *Chapter 11: Consciousness, Suffering, and the Hard Question*

11

Consciousness, Suffering, and the Hard Question

What Philosophy of Mind Tells Us About Pain, Awareness, and the Self That Hurts

"There is something it is like to suffer. That 'something' is the entire problem - and the entire point."

This chapter is going to be different from the others. We are going to leave the neuroscience behind for a while - not because it does not matter, but because there are questions about trauma and the self that neuroscience cannot fully answer. Questions about what it means that there is someone inside the experience. That trauma is not just a set of biological processes but a lived, felt reality happening to a conscious being who is aware of their own suffering.

We are going to ask philosophical questions. Not because

philosophy provides solutions - it rarely does - but because the questions themselves matter. Because how you think about consciousness, about suffering, about what it means to be a self that persists through difficulty - these are not academic puzzles. They are questions that shape how you understand your own experience, how you relate to your pain, and what you believe is possible for the person you are becoming.

This chapter is about the hard problem of consciousness: why does physical processing give rise to subjective experience at all? It is about phenomenology: what does it actually feel like, from the inside, to exist as a person carrying trauma? It is about the ethics of suffering: what does the fact of conscious experience demand of us, morally? And it is about the self - whether there is a continuous you that persists through all the fragmentation, all the dissociation, all the ways trauma tries to break you into pieces.

If this sounds abstract, stay with me. Because I am going to argue that these questions are not separate from the practical work of healing. They are foundational to it. The way you understand what consciousness is - what it means that you exist as a subject, aware of your own experience - shapes everything else. Your sense of agency. Your capacity for hope. Your belief that the person suffering now is the same person who might, someday, suffer less.

11.1 - The Hard Problem: Why Consciousness Is the Most Puzzling Thing in the Universe

In 1995, philosopher David Chalmers drew a distinction that has dominated philosophy of mind ever since. He distinguished between what he called the 'easy problems' of consciousness and the 'hard problem.'

The easy problems - and he used that term with deliberate irony, because they are not easy at all - are the problems of explaining how the brain processes information, integrates sensory data, controls behavior, reports on internal states. These are tractable scientific questions. They are enormously difficult, but they are the kind of questions that neuroscience can, in principle, answer. We can map neural pathways. We can identify which brain regions are active during which tasks. We can describe, in increasingly fine detail, the physical mechanisms of cognition.

The hard problem is something else entirely. It is the question: why does any of this physical processing give rise to subjective experience? Why is there something it is like to be you? Why does seeing red not just trigger certain neural responses, but also produce the felt quality of redness? Why does pain not just activate nociceptors and send signals to the brain, but also hurt? Why is there an inner life at all?

Why This Matters for Understanding Trauma

You might be wondering why a book about childhood trauma is spending time on abstract philosophy of mind. Here is why.

Trauma is not just a neurological event. It is not just the activation of the HPA axis, or the sensitization of the amygdala, or the dysregulation of the autonomic nervous system. All of that is true and important. But trauma is also - and this is what the hard problem points us toward - a subjective experience. It is something that hurts, from the inside. It is lived. It is felt. There is someone it is happening to.

And that someone-ness - the fact of subjectivity, the presence of a first-person perspective, the reality of lived experience - is not captured by the neuroscience alone. You can describe every neural correlate of suffering and still not have explained what it feels like to suffer. The map is not the territory. The brain state is not the conscious experience, even if they are correlated. There is an explanatory gap between the physical description and the felt reality. And that gap is where the hard problem lives.

> *The hard problem of consciousness is not an academic curiosity. It is the recognition that your suffering is real in a way that transcends its biological description. That there is a you experiencing all of this. And that matters.*

Qualia: The Felt Qualities of Experience

Philosophers use a technical term for the subjective, felt qualities of experience: qualia. The redness of red. The painfulness of pain. The particular way fear feels different from sadness, even though both are unpleasant emotions. These felt qualities are what make experience experiential. They are the 'what it is like' that Chalmers and others point to when they talk about consciousness.

And here is what is strange and important about qualia: they seem to be irreducible. You cannot fully convey what red looks like to someone who has never seen color. You cannot adequately describe what pain feels like to someone who has never felt it. There is something about subjective experience that resists third-person description. You have to be the subject to know it.

This is why trauma survivors often feel that no one who has not been through it can truly understand. Not because non-survivors are unsympathetic or unintelligent, but because the qualia of trauma - the felt texture of dissociation, the particular quality of a body that is braced for threat, the way depression changes not just mood but the entire phenomenology of time and possibility - these are not fully communicable. They have to be lived to be known.

This is not an argument for silence or isolation. It is an argument for epistemic humility. For recognizing that there is a dimension of another person's experience that you, from the outside, cannot fully access. And for honoring that privacy, that interiority, as real and significant even when it cannot be perfectly translated into shared language.

Consciousness and the Possibility of Change

Here is where the hard problem connects to the practical work of healing. If consciousness is reducible to brain states - if there is no hard problem, if subjective experience is just what information processing feels like from the inside - then changing the brain should automatically change the experience. Fix the neurology, fix the consciousness. Simple.

But if there is a hard problem - if consciousness is something more than, or at least something distinct from, the physical processes that give rise to it - then the relationship between changing the brain and changing the experience is more complex. The experience is not simply a passive reflection of brain state. It is its own reality, with its own dynamics, its own resistance to change, its own persistence even when the underlying conditions shift.

This is what many trauma survivors discover in therapy. The insight comes. The neural patterns shift. The cognitive distortions are identified and challenged. And yet the felt experience - the qualia of fear, of dissociation, of being a self that does not quite trust the world - persists. Not because the therapy failed, but because subjective experience has an inertia of its own. It is not simply read off from brain states. It is constituted by them, yes. But it is also something more. Something that has to be attended to on its own terms, in its own language, at its own pace.

11.2 - Phenomenology of Suffering: What It Actually Feels Like

Phenomenology is the branch of philosophy that studies the structures of experience from the first-person point of view. It asks: what is it like to perceive, to remember, to imagine, to feel? It is not interested in what the brain is doing during these experiences - that is neuroscience's domain. It is interested in the experience itself, described with as much precision and honesty as language allows.

And for our purposes - for understanding trauma - phenomenology offers something invaluable: a vocabulary for describing what cannot be measured. For naming the textures of experience that neuroscience leaves out.

The Texture of Fear

Let me try to describe something with phenomenological precision. Fear, from the inside.

Fear is not just an elevated heart rate or a spike in cortisol. Those are correlates. Fear, as lived experience, is a contraction. The world shrinks. The future collapses into the immediate present. Your attention narrows to the threat - or to the vigilance for threat, which is its own kind of threat. Time changes quality; it either stretches, each second feeling interminable, or it compresses, everything happening too fast to process.

Your body is no longer neutral space you inhabit. It becomes charged, alert, almost humming with readiness. You are aware of your heartbeat in a way you normally are not. Your breathing is shallow, and you notice that shallowness. There is a tightness in your chest or throat or stomach - a physical sensation that is inseparable from the emotion, so that you cannot tell whether the fear is producing the tightness or the tightness is producing the fear.

And underneath all of this, there is a kind of wrongness. The world feels different. Not in its objective features - the room is still the same room - but in its affective quality. Everything is slightly off, slightly dangerous, slightly not-right. And you, the self experiencing all this, feel both hyperalert and disoriented. Present in your body in a way that is uncomfortable, and simultaneously distant from yourself, as if watching your own fear from a small, removed vantage point.

That is what fear feels like. Not the clinical description. The lived reality. And for someone whose nervous system is chronically activated, that lived reality is not an occasional state. It is the background hum of existence.

> *The phenomenology of trauma is not what trauma does to the brain. It is what trauma feels like to a consciousness that is aware of its own suffering - and cannot simply decide to stop being aware.*

Dissociation as Phenomenological Shift

Dissociation, which we discussed in clinical terms in Chapter 4, has a phenomenology that is worth describing carefully, because it is one of the strangest alterations of consciousness that human beings regularly experience.

When you dissociate, the world does not disappear. You do not lose consciousness. But the quality of consciousness changes. There is a distance that inserts itself between you and your experience. Things that should feel real feel flat, two-dimensional, as if they are happening on a screen rather than in the world you inhabit. Your own body can feel unfamiliar, as if it belongs to someone else. Your voice sounds strange. Your movements feel automatic, disconnected from intention.

Philosopher Matthew Ratcliffe, who has written extensively on the phenomenology of depression and trauma, describes dissociation as a loss of 'existential feeling' - the pre-reflective sense of being situated in a world, of being present, of mattering. When you dissociate, that sense goes dim. You are technically present, but you do not feel present. You exist, but you do not feel real.

And here is what makes dissociation particularly disorienting: you are aware of the distance. You can observe, from that removed vantage point, that you should be feeling something and are not. That you should be present and are not quite. The consciousness is still there, still watching, but it is watching itself fail to connect. It is a strange doubling, a divided awareness that is both protective and profoundly alienating.

Time and the Loss of Futurity

One of the most profound phenomenological changes that trauma produces - particularly chronic trauma and depression - is a shift in how time itself is experienced. Not clock time. Lived time. The felt sense of past, present, and future.

In ordinary experience, the future exists as a space of possibility. It is open, not yet determined, available for shaping through your actions. This openness is what makes planning, hoping, and striving feel meaningful. The future is not just a later present. It is a different kind of thing - potential rather than actual, alive with options that have not yet collapsed into single outcomes.

In depression and chronic trauma, this sense of futurity collapses. The future does not feel open. It feels closed, predetermined, indistinguishable from the present. The heaviness you feel now will be the heaviness you feel tomorrow. The struggle is not temporary. It is permanent. Time stretches forward not as a space of possibility but as an extension of now, with all of now's difficulty, forever.

Ratcliffe calls this a 'loss of existential hope' - not hope for a specific outcome, but hope as the basic temporal structure of being-in-the-world. The felt sense that things could be different. That change is possible. That the future is genuinely future rather than just later present.

This is not a cognitive distortion you can simply argue yourself out of. It is a shift in the phenomenology of time itself. And it is one of the reasons why depression is so hard to treat, why telling someone to 'just think positive' or 'focus on the future' misses the point entirely. The future, for them, has ceased to exist as a meaningful category. There is only this, extending.

11.3 - The Ethics of Suffering: What Consciousness Demands of Us

If consciousness is real - if there is genuine subjective experience, if suffering is not just a brain state but something that is actually felt by a subject - then this has ethical implications. It means that suffering matters not just instrumentally, not just because of its effects on behavior or health, but intrinsically. Because there is someone it is happening to. And that someone's experience is morally significant.

Peter Singer and the Capacity for Suffering

Philosopher Peter Singer, best known for his work on animal ethics, makes an argument that is relevant here. He claims that the capacity for suffering is the minimum threshold for moral consideration. If a being can suffer - if there is something it is like to be that being, and that something can include pain - then that being has interests. And those interests matter morally.

This is why we have ethical obligations toward animals, Singer argues, and why those obligations are independent of intelligence, language, or any other cognitive capacity. The cow being slaughtered suffers. There is someone it is happening to. And that subjective experience of pain is morally significant in itself, regardless of whether the cow can reason about its situation or articulate its suffering in language.

Now apply this to humans. To children, specifically. A child being abused is not just a human organism being damaged. There is conscious experience happening. There is fear. There is pain. There is confusion about why the person who should be safe is hurting them. There is a subjective life that is being violated. And that subjective dimension - the fact that there is someone inside the experience - is what makes the harm not just a violation of rights or social norms, but a moral catastrophe.

This is not an abstract point. It is the reason why child abuse is worse than property damage. Why trauma is not just a health problem but an ethical problem. The consciousness is real. The suffering is real. And we have obligations - to ourselves and to others - that arise from that reality.

> *If suffering is subjectively real - if it hurts from the inside - then it is morally real. And morally real suffering makes demands on us: to prevent it when we can, to alleviate it when we cannot prevent it, and to honor it when we can do neither.*

The Obligation to Yourself

Most ethical theories focus on obligations to others. What we owe to other conscious beings who can suffer. But there is also the question of what you owe to yourself. To the conscious subject that is you, that has been carrying suffering, that continues to exist inside the difficulty.

This is not selfishness. It is a recognition that you, too, are a subject with morally significant experience. That your suffering matters. That you have the same right to relief, to care, to the conditions that make flourishing possible, that you would grant to anyone else.

For trauma survivors, this can be a difficult recognition. Because the messages you received - implicitly or explicitly - were often that your pain did not matter. That you were too sensitive, too difficult, too much. That other people's needs came first. That your job was to minimize yourself, to take up less space, to require less care. The idea that you might actually be owed something - owed care, owed attention, owed the effort it takes to heal - can feel strange. Unfamiliar. Almost presumptuous.

But if consciousness is real, if subjective experience matters morally, then it matters for you too. You are not an exception to the moral universe. The consciousness inside you that experiences pain is the same kind of consciousness as any other. And it makes the same moral demands: for care, for attention, for the alleviation of suffering when alleviation is possible.

This does not mean you can simply demand that the world fix things for you. But it does mean that you are justified in pursuing healing. That taking care of yourself is not an indulgence. That the work of therapy, of building a life that reduces suffering and increases wellbeing, is not selfish. It is a recognition of the moral significance of your own consciousness. The fact that there is someone in there, and that someone deserves to be cared for.

11.4 - The Self That Persists: Identity Through Fragmentation

We return, finally, to the question that has threaded through this entire book: who are you? More specifically: is there a continuous self that persists through all the fragmentation, all the dissociation, all the ways trauma splits experience into pieces that do not quite connect?

This is not just a philosophical question. It is a practical one. Because if the self is fundamentally fragmented, if there is no continuous you, then the question 'who is healing?' becomes strange. Who is doing the work? Who benefits from the change? If the person you were as a traumatized child and the person you are now as a recovering adult are not the same person in any meaningful sense, then what exactly is recovery?

The Witness Consciousness: The Part That Was Always Watching

Many trauma survivors describe an experience of having a part of themselves that remained intact even during the worst moments. A witness. An observer. The part that was aware of what was happening even when the rest of the self was overwhelmed, dissociated, or simply trying to survive moment to moment.

This is not the same as the whole self. The witness is not unaffected, not undamaged. But it is there. It is the part that remembers, even when memory is fragmentary. It is the part that reflects, even when reflection is painful. It is the part that kept asking questions - why is this happening, what did I do wrong, how do I make it stop, will this ever end - even when there were no good answers.

Philosophically, this witness consciousness points toward something interesting about the nature of self. It suggests that there is a minimal self - a basic sense of 'I am experiencing this' - that persists even when the richer, more narrative self is disrupted. You can lose your sense of who you are, in the bigger sense. You can lose the story of yourself. But you do not lose the bare fact of being a subject. Of being the one to whom experience is happening.

And that minimal self, that witness, is what carries through. It is the continuity. Not the narrative - the narrative can be revised, rewritten, reframed. But the fact of subjectivity itself. The fact that there is someone here, still, watching. Still asking whether change is possible. Still, against all the evidence that would suggest otherwise, continuing.

> *The self is not a fixed object. But it is also not nothing. It is the continuity of consciousness. The fact that there is someone experiencing all of this, and that someone has been you the entire time.*

Integration as Gathering the Fragments

If trauma fragments the self, then healing requires integration. Not fusion, as if the parts were entirely separate people who need to merge. But the weaving together of fragments into something that feels coherent. That feels like one person, living one life, rather than multiple selves taking turns without awareness of each other.

This is the work that therapies like Internal Family Systems explicitly target. The recognition that you have parts - a part that is angry, a part that is scared, a part that learned to people-please, a part that wants to give up - and that these parts are not separate personalities but adaptations. Strategies. Different ways the self learned to respond to different demands.

Integration does not mean those parts go away. It means they learn to communicate with each other. To recognize that they are all part of the same system, serving the same person, and that they no longer have to operate in isolation or conflict. The angry part does not have to take over completely. The scared part does not have to hide forever. They can coexist, each contributing what it knows, each holding a piece of the truth.

And underneath all the parts, there is the witness. The you that has been here the entire time. The one who is reading these words right now, wondering whether integration is possible, whether the fragments can be gathered, whether there is a way to feel whole. That witness is the self. And it has been waiting, patiently, for the rest of you to come home.

✦✦✦

Let me close this chapter with something personal, because this material is philosophical but it is also deeply intimate.

There is a particular kind of loneliness that comes with trauma. Not just the social isolation, though that is real. But the existential loneliness of having an inner experience that feels untranslatable. Of suffering in a way that you believe no one else can fully understand. Of being trapped inside a consciousness that is aware of its own difficulty and cannot simply decide to stop being aware.

The hard problem of consciousness - the fact that subjective experience is real and irreducible - means that this loneliness is, in some sense, unavoidable. No one can fully know what it is like to be you. No one can access your qualia, your phenomenology, the felt texture of your particular consciousness. You are, in that deep sense, alone inside your experience.

But - and this is crucial - that does not mean you are unknowable. It does not mean connection is impossible. It means that connection requires something more than perfect understanding. It requires empathy. Imagination. The willingness to honor what cannot be fully translated. The recognition that even though I cannot feel exactly what you feel, I can care about the fact that you feel it. I can take your subjective experience seriously. I can treat your consciousness as morally real, as significant, as worthy of care.

And you can do the same for yourself. You can recognize that your suffering is real. That there is a you experiencing it. That you have been here, conscious and witnessing, the entire time. And that self - that witness, that minimal continuous you - deserves care. Deserves the effort it takes to heal. Deserves the life that is still, despite everything, possible to build.

Consciousness Is Not the Problem - It Is the Point

This has been the most philosophically dense chapter in the book, and I am grateful if you have stayed with it. We have walked through the hard problem of consciousness and why it matters that there is a you inside all the neurology. The phenomenology of suffering - the lived, felt reality of fear, dissociation, and the collapse of futurity. The ethics of suffering and what the reality of consciousness demands morally. And the question of the self: whether there is a continuous you that persists through fragmentation, and what integration might mean.

What I hope you take from this is not a set of philosophical positions to defend, but a reframe. Consciousness is not an accident. It is not an unfortunate side effect of having a complex brain. It is what makes experience matter. It is what makes your suffering real and morally significant. It is what makes healing meaningful - because there is someone who benefits from it. You.

The neuroscience tells us what is happening in the brain. The phenomenology tells us what it feels like. The philosophy tells us why it matters that it feels like anything at all. And together, these disciplines point toward something essential: you are not just a collection of symptoms or a bundle of neural pathways. You are a conscious subject. And that subjectivity is not a weakness or a vulnerability. It is the condition of possibility for everything that matters - for suffering, yes, but also for love, for meaning, for hope, for the capacity to change.

There is one chapter left. The final chapter is about integration. About the life you build in the ruins. About becoming, slowly and imperfectly, the person you always were underneath all the adaptations and armor and survival strategies. About coming home to the self that has been waiting, patiently, to be whole.

⊠ *Chapter 12: The Life You Build in the Ruins*

12

The Life You Build in the Ruins

Integration, Wholeness, and Becoming the Person You Always Were

"You do not heal by becoming someone else. You heal by becoming more completely yourself."

We have traveled a long way together. From the house that shaped you, through the biology of fear and the fragmented self, through depression and the body that keeps the score, through the masks and the money and the compound weight of it all. And then the turn: toward resilience, toward growth, toward the possibility of loving without a map and understanding what consciousness itself tells us about suffering and the self.

Now we arrive at the final question, the one this book has been moving toward from the beginning: what does healing actually look like? Not in theory. Not as an abstract concept. But in practice. In a life. In your life.

This chapter is about integration. About gathering the fragments into something that feels whole. About building a life that honors what happened without being defined entirely by it. About becoming - slowly, imperfectly, through effort and grace and the slow accumulation of better days - the person you were always capable of being.

I want to be clear from the start: I am not going to tell you that healing is linear, or quick, or that there is a moment when you are suddenly fixed. Recovery from complex trauma is not a destination. It is a direction. A set of practices, relationships, and choices that, over time, make life feel more liveable. More yours. Less like something happening to you and more like something you are participating in shaping.

And I want to say, before we begin, that if you have made it this far - through eleven chapters of difficult material, through the recognition of patterns you carry, through the weight of seeing clearly what trauma has cost - you are already doing the work. Reading is work. Understanding is work. The willingness to look at yourself honestly, without flinching, without immediately defending or dismissing - that is some of the hardest work there is. And you are doing it. So before we talk about what comes next, I want you to know: you have already begun.

12.1 - What Integration Actually Means

Integration is one of those words that gets used in therapeutic contexts but rarely defined with precision. So let me be clear about what I mean when I use it.

Integration is not the erasure of trauma. It is not going back to some imagined pre-trauma state of innocence or wholeness. You cannot unlearn what you know. You cannot undo what happened. The experiences are part of your history. The neural pathways were formed. The body remembers.

Integration is also not simply accepting what happened and moving on, as if trauma were something you file away in a drawer labeled 'dealt with' and never think about again. Trauma does not work that way. It resurfaces. It echoes. It shows up in your relationships, your nervous system, your body, often when you least expect it.

What integration means is this: the traumatic experiences become part of your life story without being the whole story. The memories, when they surface, can be held without completely overwhelming you. The parts of yourself that developed as survival strategies - the hypervigilance, the people-pleasing, the dissociation - can be recognized for what they are: adaptations that made sense, that you can be grateful to, and that you no longer need to rely on exclusively.

Integration means you have access to yourself. All of yourself. The part that is angry can exist alongside the part that wants connection. The part that is scared can coexist with the part that is brave. The wounded child and the competent adult are both real, both present, and they can communicate rather than existing in isolated compartments that do not know about each other.

> *Integration is not becoming someone new. It is becoming less divided. Less at war with yourself. More able to be one person, living one life, rather than a collection of parts taking turns without coordination.*

The Witness Gathers the Fragments

In Chapter 11, we talked about the witness consciousness - the part of you that has been present the entire time, watching, aware, even when the rest of the self was fragmented or dissociated. Integration is, in a sense, the witness finally being able to see all the parts clearly. To hold them all in awareness at the same time. To recognize that they are all you.

This is the work that therapies like Internal Family Systems focus on explicitly: helping you develop what IFS calls 'Self' - the calm, compassionate, curious center from which you can observe and relate to all your parts without being overtaken by any single one. The angry part does not have to dominate. The scared part does not have to hide. They can all be present, and you - the capital-S Self, the witness - can hold space for all of them.

This is a radically different relationship to your internal experience than the one you may have now. Right now, you might feel taken over by emotions. Flooded by them. Or you might feel nothing, shut down, dissociated. Integration is the middle ground: you feel what you feel, but you are not only what you feel. You can be angry without being consumed by anger. You can be sad without drowning in sadness. You can be scared without fleeing or freezing.

This capacity develops slowly. Through therapy. Through mindfulness practices that teach you to observe your thoughts and feelings without identifying completely with them. Through the deliberate practice of noticing when a part is activated and pausing long enough to ask: what does this part need? What is it trying to protect me from? And what would it be like to let it know that I am safe now, that the threat it is guarding against is no longer present?

The parts do not go away. They just stop running the show. They become advisors rather than dictators. And you, the witness, become the one making decisions. Not perfectly. Not all the time. But more and more often. Until eventually, it feels more natural to be whole than to be fragmented. To be integrated than to be at war.

12.2 - The Practices That Support Integration

Integration does not happen by accident. It requires deliberate effort, sustained over time. Not because you are broken and need fixing, but because the patterns you developed have been reinforced for years or decades, and changing them requires new patterns to be practiced until they become automatic.

What follows are not prescriptions. They are options. Tools that research and clinical experience have shown to be effective for many people. Not all of them will work for you. Not all of them will be accessible to you. But some of them will. And the ones that work are worth investing in.

Therapy That Actually Addresses Trauma

Not all therapy is trauma therapy. And if you are carrying complex trauma from childhood, standard talk therapy - while valuable for many things - is often not sufficient. What you need is therapy that specifically addresses how trauma is stored in the brain and body, and that provides tools for working with it.

The modalities that have the strongest evidence base for treating complex trauma include EMDR (Eye Movement Desensitization and Reprocessing), which helps reprocess traumatic memories so they become less vivid and intrusive; Somatic Experiencing, which works directly with the body's defensive responses; Internal Family Systems, which helps you develop a compassionate relationship with all your parts; and trauma-focused CBT, which addresses the thought patterns and beliefs that trauma created.

What matters more than the specific modality is finding a therapist who understands trauma, who can provide a stable and safe relationship over time, and who is skilled at helping you work with overwhelming material without becoming retraumatized by it. This is not easy to find. Good trauma therapists are in high demand, often expensive, and not always accessible. But if therapy is within reach for you, it is worth the effort to find someone who actually knows what they are doing.

And if therapy is not accessible - financially, geographically, or for other reasons - know that it is not the only pathway. People heal through relationships, through spiritual practice, through creative work, through community. Therapy is powerful, but it is not the only tool.

The Body as Ally: Movement, Breath, and Somatic Practice

We talked in Chapter 6 about the body that keeps the score. Integration requires bringing the body back into the process. Not as an enemy to be disciplined or controlled, but as an ally that carries wisdom you cannot access through thought alone.

Practices that help include trauma-sensitive yoga, which teaches you to inhabit your body safely; breathwork, particularly techniques that emphasize slow, deep breathing to activate the parasympathetic nervous system; mindful movement like tai chi, qigong, or simply walking with attention; and any form of exercise that you can do with presence rather than dissociation.

The key is not intensity. It is attention. You are not trying to exhaust yourself or prove how strong you are. You are trying to reconnect with a body that trauma taught you to leave. To feel sensations without immediately interpreting them as danger. To notice where tension lives and experiment with releasing it.

To learn, slowly, that being in your body is something you can tolerate - and eventually, something you might even enjoy.

The Regulation: Co-Regulation and Connection

One of the most powerful tools for healing trauma is something that cannot be done alone: relationship. Specifically, relationships with people whose nervous systems are regulated enough to help regulate yours. This is co-regulation, which we have discussed before, but which is worth emphasizing again because it is so important.

Your nervous system learns from other nervous systems. If you spend time with someone who is calm, present, and emotionally available, your nervous system begins to entrain to theirs. Over time, through repeated experiences of safe connection, your system learns that not everyone is a threat. That closeness can be safe. That you can let your guard down without being harmed.

This can happen in therapy. It can happen in a romantic relationship with a securely attached partner. It can happen in friendships where you allow yourself to be seen. It can happen in support groups where you realize you are not the only one carrying what you carry. The specific context matters less than the quality of the connection: consistent, safe, non-judgmental, and present.

For many trauma survivors, this is the hardest recommendation to follow, because relationships are precisely what trauma made difficult. If you are not ready for this yet, that is fine. Start small. Start where you are. Even brief, low-stakes interactions with people who are safe can begin to shift the nervous system. The barista who smiles. The neighbor who waves. The online community where you feel less alone. Every positive interaction is data. Every experience of being seen without being harmed is evidence.

Meaning-Making and Narrative Work

Integration requires a story. Not the story you were told about yourself by people who hurt you. Not the story that shame tells you. But a story that is true. That acknowledges what happened, what it cost, and also what you have done with it. The resilience you have shown. The person you are becoming.

This is the work of narrative therapy, but it is also something you can do outside formal therapy. Through journaling. Through conversations with people you trust. Through creative work - writing, art, music - that allows you to externalize and examine your experience. Through the deliberate act of reflecting on your life and asking: what is the story I am telling about myself? Is it true? Is it complete? What parts am I leaving out?

The goal is not to create a story where trauma was a gift or where suffering was necessary for growth. The goal is to create a story where trauma is one part of a larger life. Where you are not defined entirely by what was done to you, but also by what you have done with it. Where the past is acknowledged as real and significant, but the future is still open. Where you are the author, not the subject. The agent, not the victim.

> *The story you tell about yourself is not just description. It is construction. It shapes who you believe you are and what you believe is possible. Tell a story that honors the truth - and also honors your agency.*

12.3 - What a Good Life Actually Looks Like After Trauma

Let me be very honest about something that I think is important to say clearly.

A good life after trauma does not look like a life where trauma never happened. It does not look like perfect mental health, perfect relationships, perfect stability. Those things are not realistic for anyone, and certainly not for someone whose early years were spent in survival mode.

A good life after trauma looks like this: you have days that are hard, but they do not destroy you. You have relationships that are imperfect, but they are real and you can mostly stay present in them. You have work that is meaningful enough to be worth doing, even if it is not always easy. You have moments - some of them brief, some of them sustained - where you feel okay. Where you are not fighting yourself or the world. Where you can rest.

It looks like knowing your triggers and having strategies for managing them. It looks like being able to ask for help when you need it. It looks like having one or two people in your life who know your history and have stayed. It looks like being able to tolerate discomfort without immediately dissociating or numbing. It looks like having hobbies, interests, things you do just because you enjoy them, not because they are useful or productive.

It looks like this: you are not happy all the time, but you are not in crisis all the time either. You have built a life that is stable enough to hold you. And most days, that feels like enough.

The Modest Goals of Recovery

Recovery from complex trauma is not about achieving some ideal state of wellness. It is about expanding what psychologists call your window of tolerance - the range of emotional intensity you can handle without becoming overwhelmed or shut down. When you start, that window might be very narrow. A small stressor sends you into hyperarousal or dissociation. As you heal, the window widens. You can handle more before you lose your regulation. You come back to baseline faster when you do get dysregulated.

The goals are modest, but they matter enormously. Being able to have a difficult conversation without shutting down. Being able to feel anger without it becoming rage. Being able to feel sadness without it becoming despair. Being able to need someone without it becoming terror. These are not small achievements. For someone whose nervous system was shaped by trauma, these are enormous.

And the goal is not perfection. It is direction. You are not aiming to never be triggered, never struggle, never have a bad day. You are aiming to have more good days than bad ones. To recover faster when you do get knocked off balance. To know, even in the difficult moments, that they will pass. That you have survived difficulty before and will survive it again.

Rest Is Not Weakness

One of the hardest lessons for trauma survivors to learn - and I include myself in this - is that rest is not weakness. That you do not have to earn the right to stop working, stop performing, stop proving your worth.

For people who grew up in environments where love was conditional on usefulness, where value was tied to productivity, where rest was punished or unavailable, the idea of simply existing without justification feels strange. Wrong. Almost immoral. There is a voice that says: you have not done enough. You have not earned this. You should be doing more.

That voice is the trauma. It is the internalized message from an environment that never gave you permission to simply be. And part of healing is learning to recognize that voice, to understand where it came from, and to gently, firmly, tell it: I do not have to earn rest. I am allowed to be tired. I am allowed to stop. My worth is not measured by my productivity. I am enough, just as I am.

This does not happen overnight. The belief is too deep, the pattern too old. But you can practice. You can take one day where you do less than you think you should and see what happens. You can sit with the discomfort of not being productive and notice that nothing catastrophic occurs. You can, slowly, teach yourself that rest is not a luxury or a reward. It is a biological necessity. And you, like every other living thing, are entitled to it.

Joy Is Not Betrayal

There is a particular guilt that many trauma survivors carry: the guilt of feeling good. Of having a moment of joy, or peace, or simple contentment, and immediately feeling like you do not deserve it. Like you are betraying the child you were, who suffered. Like happiness is not something you have earned or are allowed to keep.

This guilt is understandable. But it is not accurate. Feeling good now does not erase what happened then. Allowing yourself joy does not dishonor the pain you carried. In fact, the opposite is true: the best way to honor the child who survived is to let the adult you are now have the things that child never had. Safety. Rest. Connection. The permission to exist without constant vigilance. The experience of being in a body that feels okay.

Joy is not betrayal. It is reclamation. It is proof that the trauma did not win. That you are still here, still capable of feeling, still capable of building a life that is worth living. The child who survived deserves that. And so do you.

12.4 - The Person You Are Becoming

Integration is not a destination. It is a process. And the process does not end. You do not arrive at a point where you are fully healed, fully integrated, fully complete and never have to think about any of this again.

What happens instead is that you become someone who is actively engaged in the process of becoming. Someone who is learning, still. Growing, still. Changing, still. But doing so with more awareness, more agency, more choice than you had before.

You become someone who knows your patterns well enough to see them operating. Who can catch yourself in the act of people-pleasing, or hypervigilance, or dissociation, and pause long enough to ask: is this serving me right now? Is this what I actually want to be doing, or is this just what I learned to do?

You become someone who can recognize when your nervous system is dysregulated and has tools to bring it back to baseline. Who knows what co-regulation feels like and can seek it out when you need it. Who can tell the difference between a threat response and an actual threat, and who can - not always, but increasingly - respond to the present rather than reacting to the past.

You become someone who can hold complexity. Who can acknowledge that the trauma was real and shaped you, and also that you are not only the trauma. Who can be angry about what happened and also grateful for what you learned. Who can grieve what was lost and also celebrate what was built from the ruins.

> *The person you are becoming is not someone new. It is the person you always were, underneath all the adaptations and armor. It is the self you would have been if the world had been kinder. And it is the self you are choosing to be now, despite everything.*

The Quiet Triumph of an Ordinary Life

There is a particular kind of heroism in the way trauma survivors live. Not the dramatic kind that gets recognized or celebrated. But the quiet kind. The kind that shows up every day to a life that is harder than it should be and keeps going anyway.

Getting out of bed when depression says to stay there. Going to work when your body hurts and your mind is exhausted. Showing up for relationships when relationships have always been difficult. Doing the dishes. Paying the bills. Making dinner. Answering emails. All the mundane, ordinary tasks of adult life that are monumentally difficult when you are carrying what you are carrying.

No one gives you credit for this. No one sees the effort it takes. From the outside, you look like everyone else. Functional. Fine. Getting by. What they do not see is the sheer force of will it requires some days just to exist. The work of staying present in your body. The work of not giving up. The work of continuing to believe, even on days when belief feels impossible, that the future might be different from the past.

That is the quiet triumph. Not achieving something extraordinary. Just achieving the ordinary, when the ordinary was never guaranteed. Building a life that is not defined by trauma even though trauma is part of it. Becoming someone who can love, and work, and rest, and exist without constant crisis. That is the victory. And it is worth everything it cost.

You Are Already Whole

Let me close with something that might seem paradoxical, given everything this book has been about.

You are not broken. You never were. The way you adapted to an impossible situation was not a defect. It was intelligence. It was survival. It was the best you could do with what you had, and it was enough. You made it. You are here.

Integration is not about fixing something broken. It is about recognizing that the self that survived - with all its fragments, all its strategies, all its scars - is the self that kept you alive. And that self is not deficient. It is extraordinary.

What you are doing now is not becoming whole. You were always whole. You are becoming more integrated, yes. More present, yes. More able to access all of yourself rather than just the parts that were safe to show. But you were never broken. You were shaped by difficult circumstances. And the shape you took made sense.

The work is not to become someone else. It is to become more completely yourself. To shed the armour that is no longer needed. To let the parts that were hidden come into the light. To allow the person you were before the world told you who to be – the person who has been waiting patiently all this time – to finally, finally, be seen.

That person is you. Not a future version. Not a fixed version. Just you, as you are, minus the weight of carrying what was never yours to carry. That is who you are becoming. And they are worth every effort it takes to get there.

✦✦✦

We have reached the end of this book. But not the end of the journey. The journey continues. For as long as you are alive, you are still becoming. Still learning. Still gathering the fragments. Still building the life that is yours.

I hope this book has given you something useful. Not answers – there are no final answers to questions this complex. But clarity, perhaps. Context. The science that explains what you have lived. The philosophy that honors what it has meant to live it. The recognition that you are not alone in this. That others have walked this path and found it possible to build something good at the end of it.

If you take nothing else from these pages, take this: you were shaped by trauma, but you are not defined by it. You carry wounds, but you are not only wounded. You have survived, and survival – just survival, just being here, just continuing to exist through everything that tried to break you - is already a form of strength that most people will never have to develop.

The fact that you picked up a book about childhood trauma and read all the way to the end tells me something about you. It tells me you are still asking questions. Still seeking understanding. Still believing, on some level, that change is possible. And that belief, fragile as it might feel, is the foundation of everything that comes next.

You do not need to have it all figured out. You do not need to be healed before you are allowed to rest. You are allowed to be exactly where you are right now - struggling, hopeful, exhausted, still going - and that is enough. You are enough.

The life you build from here is yours. Not perfect. Not unmarked by what came before. But yours. Built by you. Shaped by your choices, your effort, your refusal to let trauma be the final word. That life is worth building. And you are worth the effort it takes.

Thank you for reading. Thank you for making it this far. And thank you for continuing, despite everything, to be.

- END -

IV

Calculate Your ACE Score

Understanding Your Score and What It Means

13

Adverse Childhood Experiences (ACE) Assessment

13.1 - What Is the ACE Score?

The Adverse Childhood Experiences (ACE) Study, conducted by the CDC and Kaiser Permanente from 1995 to 1997, examined the relationship between childhood trauma and adult health outcomes. The study surveyed over 17,000 participants and established clear correlations between early adversity and later physical and mental health.

Your ACE score is a count of the different types of adversity you experienced before the age of 18. Each category of experience counts as one point. The higher the score, the greater the statistical correlation with certain health outcomes - but it is important to understand that this is correlation, not destiny. Many people with high ACE scores lead healthy, fulfilling lives. The score is a tool for understanding, not a verdict.

13.2 - Calculate Your ACE Score

Before the age of 18, did you experience any of the following? For each YES answer, add one point to your score. Answer honestly - this is for your understanding only.

Category 1: Abuse

1. Emotional Abuse: *Did a parent or adult in your home often swear at you, insult you, put you down, or humiliate you? Or act in a way that made you afraid you might be physically hurt?*

2. Physical Abuse: *Did a parent or adult in your home often push, grab, slap, or throw something at you? Or ever hit you so hard that you had marks or were injured?*

3. Sexual Abuse: *Did an adult or person at least 5 years older than you ever touch or fondle you or have you touch their body in a sexual way? Or try to or actually have oral, anal, or vaginal sex with you?*

Category 2: Neglect

4. Emotional Neglect: *Did you often feel that no one in your family loved you or thought you were important or special? Or that your family didn't look out for each other, feel close to each other, or support each other?*

5. Physical Neglect: *Did you often feel that you didn't have enough to eat, had to wear dirty clothes, or had no one to protect you? Or that your parents were too drunk or high to take care of* *you or take you to the doctor if you needed it?*

Category 3: Household Dysfunction

6. Mother Treated Violently: *Was your mother or stepmother often pushed, grabbed, slapped, had something thrown at her, kicked, bitten, hit with a fist, or hit with something hard? Or ever repeatedly hit over at least a few minutes or threatened with a gun or knife?*

7. Substance Abuse: *Did you live with anyone who was a problem drinker or alcoholic, or who used street drugs?*

8. Mental Illness in Household: *Was a household member depressed or mentally ill, or did a household member attempt suicide?*

9. Parental Separation or Divorce: *Were your parents ever separated or divorced?*

10. Incarcerated Household Member: *Did a household member go to prison?*

YOUR ACE SCORE: Write Score in your notebook (Total number of YES answers, 0-10)

13.3 - Understanding Your Score

The ACE Study found clear dose-response relationships: the higher the ACE score, the greater the statistical risk for certain health and social outcomes. However - and this is crucial - correlation is not causation, and statistics describe populations, not individuals. Your ACE score is a piece of information, not a destiny.

ACE Score: 0

A score of zero indicates that you did not experience any of the ten categories of childhood adversity measured by the ACE questionnaire. This does not mean your childhood was perfect or that you have not faced other challenges, but statistically, you have a lower baseline risk for the health outcomes associated with early adversity.

> *Note: People with ACE scores of 0 serve as the baseline comparison group in the research. Their outcomes represent what is statistically typical when childhood adversity (as measured by these ten categories) is absent.*

ACE Score: 1-3

About half the population falls into this range. While any childhood adversity carries some impact, scores in this range are associated with modest increases in risk compared to a score of 0. The research shows:

- *Depression risk increases by 30-50% compared to ACE score of 0*

- *Slightly elevated risk for substance use and chronic health conditions*
- *Many people in this range function well with appropriate support and self-care*

> *Important: A score in this range suggests some biological and psychological impact, but the majority of people with these scores lead healthy, productive lives. Awareness and appropriate intervention can significantly mitigate risks.*

ACE Score: 4 or Higher

About one in six adults has an ACE score of 4 or higher. This is where the statistical correlations become more pronounced and clinically significant. The research findings include:

- ***Depression**: 4–5 times higher risk than ACE score of 0*
- *Suicide attempts: 12 times higher risk*
- ***Alcoholism**: 7 times higher risk*
- *Illicit drug use: 10 times higher risk*
- ***Chronic Obstructive Pulmonary Disease (COPD)**: 4 times higher risk*
- ***Heart disease**: 2–3 times higher risk*
- ***Liver disease**: 2 times higher risk*

> *Critical context: These are population-level statistics. They describe increased risk, not certainty. Many people with high ACE scores never develop these conditions, particularly when they have access to supportive relationships, therapy, and informed self-care.*

ACE Score: 6 or Higher

Approximately one in ten adults has an ACE score of 6 or higher. This level of childhood adversity is associated with the most significant health impacts:

- *Life expectancy reduced by approximately 20 years compared to ACE score of 0*
- *Dramatically elevated risk for mental health disorders, particularly depression, PTSD, and substance use disorders*
- *Significantly higher rates of autoimmune disorders, chronic pain, and inflammatory conditions*
- *Greater likelihood of relationship difficulties, employment instability, and intergenerational transmission of adversity*

> *If you have a score of 6 or higher, please know: the statistics are sobering, but they are not your personal future. With appropriate trauma-informed care, supportive relationships, and the biological reality of neuroplasticity, significant healing is possible. Many people with high ACE scores have rebuilt their lives, their health, and their sense of wholeness. You are reading this book, which means you are already engaged in that process.*

13.4 - What the ACE Score Does Not Measure

The original ACE questionnaire, while groundbreaking, has important limitations. It does not capture:

- *Peer victimization, bullying, or community violence*
- *Racism, discrimination, or systemic oppression*
- *Poverty, food insecurity, or housing instability*

- *Witnessing violence outside the home*
- *Losing a parent to death (rather than divorce/separation)*
- *Foster care, adoption trauma, or frequent moves*

If you experienced significant adversity not captured by the ten ACE categories, your score may underrepresent your actual childhood stress exposure. Expanded ACE questionnaires exist that include these additional categories, and you may find them more comprehensive.

13.5 - What to Do With This Information

Knowing your ACE score is not about labeling yourself or accepting a predetermined outcome. It is about understanding. Here is what this information can do for you:

1. **It Explains, Not Excuses:** Your score provides context for patterns you may have noticed: difficulty with relationships, chronic health issues, struggles with emotion regulation, substance use, or depression. These are not character flaws. They are predictable consequences of early adversity, grounded in biology and neuroscience.
2. **It Guides Intervention**: If you have a high ACE score, you may benefit from trauma-informed care - therapy approaches like EMDR, somatic experiencing, or trauma-focused CBT that specifically address how trauma is stored in the brain and body. Standard approaches that do not account for trauma history are less effective.
3. **It Validates Your Experience**: For many people, seeing their childhood quantified in this way is the first time they have had external validation that what they lived through

was genuinely difficult and has had real, measurable consequences. This validation matters.

4. **It Motivates Prevention**: Understanding the health risks associated with high ACE scores can motivate proactive health behaviors: regular exercise, stress management, maintaining social connections, avoiding substance abuse, and getting regular medical care. Knowledge is power when it leads to action.
5. **It Reminds You:** This Is Not Your Fault. Whatever your score, the adversity you experienced was not something you chose, caused, or deserved. Children are not responsible for the environments they grow up in. And adults are not to blame for the biology those environments created.

13.6 - A Final Word

The ACE Study was revolutionary because it made visible what had always been invisible: the biological pathway from childhood adversity to adult illness. But the study was never meant to be a life sentence. It was meant to be a call to action - for individuals, for clinicians, for public health.

If your score is high, please hear this: the statistics describe populations, not destinies. The brain is plastic. The body can heal. Relationships can be learned. The person you are now is not the final version of who you will be. This book exists because change is possible.

And you are reading it, which means you are already on that path.

References

Books and Foundational Texts

- Ainsworth, M. D. S., Blehar, M. C., Waters, E., & Wall, S. (1978). Patterns of attachment: A psychological study of the strange situation. Lawrence Erlbaum Associates.
- Bowlby, J. (1969). Attachment and loss: Vol. 1. Attachment. Basic Books.
- Bowlby, J. (1973). Attachment and loss: Vol. 2. Separation: Anxiety and anger. Basic Books.
- Bowlby, J. (1980). Attachment and loss: Vol. 3. Loss: Sadness and depression. Basic Books.
- Chalmers, D. J. (1996). The conscious mind: In search of a fundamental theory. Oxford University Press.
- Crawford, M. B. (2009). Shop class as soulcraft: An inquiry into the value of work. Penguin Press.
- Frankl, V. E. (1946/2006). Man's search for meaning. Beacon Press.
- Goffman, E. (1959). The presentation of self in everyday life. Anchor Books.
- Levine, P. A. (1997). Waking the tiger: Healing trauma. North Atlantic Books.
- Mullainathan, S., & Shafir, E. (2013). Scarcity: Why having too little means so much. Times Books.

- Porges, S. W. (2011). The polyvagal theory: Neurophysiological foundations of emotions, attachment, communication, and self-regulation. W. W. Norton & Company.
- Ratcliffe, M. (2015). Experiences of depression: A study in phenomenology. Oxford University Press.
- Sapolsky, R. M. (2004). Why zebras don't get ulcers (3rd ed.). Henry Holt and Company.
- Schwartz, R. C. (1995). Internal family systems therapy. Guilford Press.
- Seligman, M. E. P. (1972). Learned helplessness. Annual Review of Medicine, 23(1), 407-412.
- Siegel, D. J. (1999). The developing mind: How relationships and the brain interact to shape who we are. Guilford Press.
- Singer, P. (1975). Animal liberation: A new ethics for our treatment of animals. Random House.
- Tedeschi, R. G., & Calhoun, L. G. (1995). Trauma and transformation: Growing in the aftermath of suffering. Sage Publications.
- Van der Kolk, B. A. (2014). The body keeps the score: Brain, mind, and body in the healing of trauma. Viking.
- Winnicott, D. W. (1965). The maturational processes and the facilitating environment: Studies in the theory of emotional development. International Universities Press.

Research Articles and Empirical Studies

- Anda, R. F., Felitti, V. J., Bremner, J. D., Walker, J. D., Whitfield, C., Perry, B. D., Dube, S. R., & Giles, W. H. (2006). The enduring effects of abuse and related adverse experiences in childhood: A convergence of evidence from neurobiology and epidemiology. European Archives of Psychiatry and Clinical Neuroscience, 256(3), 174-186.

- Danese, A., & McEwen, B. S. (2012). Adverse childhood experiences, allostasis, allostatic load, and age-related disease. Physiology & Behavior, 106(1), 29-39.
- Felitti, V. J., Anda, R. F., Nordenberg, D., Williamson, D. F., Spitz, A. M., Edwards, V., Koss, M. P., & Marks, J. S. (1998). Relationship of childhood abuse and household dysfunction to many of the leading causes of death in adults: The Adverse Childhood Experiences (ACE) Study. American Journal of Preventive Medicine, 14(4), 245-258.
- Hair, N. L., Hanson, J. L., Wolfe, B. L., & Pollak, S. D. (2015). Association of child poverty, brain development, and academic achievement. JAMA Pediatrics, 169(9), 822-829.
- Hebb, D. O. (1949). The organization of behavior: A neuropsychological theory. Wiley.
- Kohler, C. A., Freitas, T. H., Maes, M., de Andrade, N. Q., Liu, C. S., Fernandes, B. S., Stubbs, B., Solmi, M., Veronese, N., Herrmann, N., Raison, C. L., Miller, B. J., Lanctôt, K. L., & Carvalho, A. F. (2017). Peripheral cytokine and chemokine alterations in depression: A meta-analysis of 82 studies. Acta Psychiatrica Scandinavica, 135(5), 373-387.
- Kuhlman, K. R., Horn, S. R., Chiang, J. J., & Bower, J. E. (2017). Early life adversity exposure and circulating markers of inflammation in children and adolescents: A systematic review and meta-analysis. Brain, Behavior, and Immunity, 69, 50-61.
- Lanius, R. A., Vermetten, E., Loewenstein, R. J., Brand, B., Schmahl, C., Bremner, J. D., & Spiegel, D. (2010). Emotion modulation in PTSD: Clinical and neurobiological evidence

for a dissociative subtype. American Journal of Psychiatry, 167(6), 640-647.

- LeDoux, J. E. (1996). The emotional brain: The mysterious underpinnings of emotional life. Simon & Schuster.
- Main, M., & Solomon, J. (1986). Discovery of an insecure-disorganized/disoriented attachment pattern. In T. B. Brazelton & M. W. Yogman (Eds.), Affective development in infancy (pp. 95-124). Ablex.
- McEwen, B. S. (2007). Physiology and neurobiology of stress and adaptation: Central role of the brain. Physiological Reviews, 87(3), 873-904.
- McCrory, E., De Brito, S. A., & Viding, E. (2011). The impact of childhood maltreatment: A review of neurobiological and genetic factors. Frontiers in Psychiatry, 2, 48.
- Meaney, M. J. (2001). Maternal care, gene expression, and the transmission of individual differences in stress reactivity across generations. Annual Review of Neuroscience, 24, 1161-1192.
- Pennebaker, J. W. (1997). Writing about emotional experiences as a therapeutic process. Psychological Science, 8(3), 162-166.
- Perry, B. D., Pollard, R. A., Blakley, T. L., Baker, W. L., & Vigilante, D. (1995). Childhood trauma, the neurobiology of adaptation, and 'use-dependent' development of the brain: How 'states' become 'traits'. Infant Mental Health Journal, 16(4), 271-291.
- Shonkoff, J. P., Garner, A. S., Committee on Psychosocial Aspects of Child and Family Health, Committee on Early Childhood, Adoption, and Dependent Care, & Section on Developmental and Behavioral Pediatrics. (2012). The lifelong effects of early childhood adversity and toxic

stress. Pediatrics, 129(1), e232-e246.

- Teicher, M. H., & Samson, J. A. (2016). Annual research review: Enduring neurobiological effects of childhood abuse and neglect. Journal of Child Psychology and Psychiatry, 57(3), 241-266.
- Van IJzendoorn, M. H., Schuengel, C., & Bakermans-Kranenburg, M. J. (1999). Disorganized attachment in early childhood: Meta-analysis of precursors, concomitants, and sequelae. Development and Psychopathology, 11(2), 225-250.
- Van der Kolk, B. A., Stone, L., West, J., Rhodes, A., Emerson, D., Suvak, M., & Spinazzola, J. (2014). Yoga as an adjunctive treatment for posttraumatic stress disorder: A randomized controlled trial. Journal of Clinical Psychiatry, 75(6), e559-e565.

Neuroscience and Neuroplasticity

- Davidson, R. J., & McEwen, B. S. (2012). Social influences on neuroplasticity: Stress and interventions to promote well-being. Nature Neuroscience, 15(5), 689-695.
- Doidge, N. (2007). The brain that changes itself: Stories of personal triumph from the frontiers of brain science. Viking.
- Eriksson, P. S., Perfilieva, E., Björk-Eriksson, T., Alborn, A. M., Nordborg, C., Peterson, D. A., & Gage, F. H. (1998). Neurogenesis in the adult human hippocampus. Nature Medicine, 4(11), 1313-1317.
- Friston, K. (2010). The free-energy principle: A unified brain theory? Nature Reviews Neuroscience, 11(2), 127-138.

- Kolb, B., & Whishaw, I. Q. (1998). Brain plasticity and behavior. Annual Review of Psychology, 49, 43-64.
- Lupien, S. J., McEwen, B. S., Gunnar, M. R., & Heim, C. (2009). Effects of stress throughout the lifespan on the brain, behaviour and cognition. Nature Reviews Neuroscience, 10(6), 434-445.

Attachment and Developmental Psychology

- Cassidy, J., & Shaver, P. R. (Eds.). (2016). Handbook of attachment: Theory, research, and clinical applications (3rd ed.). Guilford Press.
- Earls, L., Bayfield, C., & Lothian, J. (2021). Earned secure attachment: A qualitative study of the long-term outcomes of attachment-based psychotherapy with adults. Attachment & Human Development, 23(6), 831-853.
- Fonagy, P., Gergely, G., Jurist, E. L., & Target, M. (2002). Affect regulation, mentalization, and the development of the self. Other Press.
- Hesse, E. (2008). The adult attachment interview: Protocol, method of analysis, and empirical studies. In J. Cassidy & P. R. Shaver (Eds.), Handbook of attachment: Theory, research, and clinical applications (2nd ed., pp. 552-598). Guilford Press.
- Mikulincer, M., & Shaver, P. R. (2007). Attachment in adulthood: Structure, dynamics, and change. Guilford Press.

Philosophy of Mind and Consciousness

- Hume, D. (1739/1978). A treatise of human nature (L. A. Selby-Bigge, Ed., 2nd ed.). Oxford University Press.
- Locke, J. (1689/1975). An essay concerning human understanding (P. H. Nidditch, Ed.). Oxford University Press.
- Nagel, T. (1974). What is it like to be a bat? The Philosophical Review, 83(4), 435-450.
- Nagel, T. (1979). Mortal questions. Cambridge University Press.
- Parfit, D. (1984). Reasons and persons. Oxford University Press.
- Stoicism and Existential Philosophy
- Epictetus. (c. 108 CE/1983). The handbook (Enchiridion) (N. P. White, Trans.). Hackett Publishing.
- Heidegger, M. (1927/1962). Being and time (J. Macquarrie & E. Robinson, Trans.). Harper & Row.
- Marcus Aurelius. (c. 170-180 CE/2006). Meditations (M. Hammond, Trans.). Penguin Classics.
- Seneca, L. A. (c. 65 CE/2004). Letters from a stoic (R. Campbell, Trans.). Penguin Classics.

Psychoneuroimmunology and Somatic Health

- Ader, R., & Cohen, N. (1975). Behaviorally conditioned immunosuppression. Psychosomatic Medicine, 37(4), 333-340.
- Cohen, S., Janicki-Deverts, D., & Miller, G. E. (2007). Psychological stress and disease. JAMA, 298(14), 1685-1687.
- Epel, E. S., Blackburn, E. H., Lin, J., Dhabhar, F. S., Adler,

N. E., Morrow, J. D., & Cawthon, R. M. (2004). Accelerated telomere shortening in response to life stress. Proceedings of the National Academy of Sciences, 101(49), 17312-17315.

- Kiecolt-Glaser, J. K., McGuire, L., Robles, T. F., & Glaser, R. (2002). Emotions, morbidity, and mortality: New perspectives from psychoneuroimmunology. Annual Review of Psychology, 53, 83-107.

Depression and Mental Health Research

- Gotlib, I. H., & Hammen, C. L. (Eds.). (2014). Handbook of depression (3rd ed.). Guilford Press.
- Kendler, K. S., Karkowski, L. M., & Prescott, C. A. (1999). Causal relationship between stressful life events and the onset of major depression. American Journal of Psychiatry, 156(6), 837-841.
- Nolen-Hoeksema, S., Wisco, B. E., & Lyubomirsky, S. (2008). Rethinking rumination. Perspectives on Psychological Science, 3(5), 400-424.

Class, Sociology, and Economics

- Bourdieu, P. (1986). The forms of capital. In J. Richardson (Ed.), Handbook of theory and research for the sociology of education (pp. 241-258). Greenwood.
- Lareau, A. (2011). Unequal childhoods: Class, race, and family life (2nd ed.). University of California Press.

Trauma Treatment Modalities

- Shapiro, F. (2001). Eye movement desensitization and reprocessing (EMDR): Basic principles, protocols, and procedures (2nd ed.). Guilford Press.
- Ogden, P., Minton, K., & Pain, C. (2006). Trauma and the body: A sensorimotor approach to psychotherapy. W. W. Norton & Company.
- Herman, J. L. (1992). Trauma and recovery: The aftermath of violence-from domestic abuse to political terror. Basic Books.

Note: This reference list includes the major sources cited throughout the text. Additional research papers, review articles, and meta-analyses informed the content but are not individually listed. Readers interested in exploring specific topics in greater depth are encouraged to consult the reference sections of the key works listed above.

About the Author

Bilal Iqbal is a thinker, dreamer, and Biotechnology student from Faisalabad, Punjab, Pakistan. Also earned Certificate of Science of Stem Cells from American Museum of Nature History. Fascinated since childhood by the night sky, biology, and the question of what it means to be human in an infinite universe, he spent years reading everything from CRISPR papers to philosophical texts on consciousness.

www.ingramcontent.com/pod-product-compliance
Lightning Source LLC
La Vergne TN
LVHW100257210926
848480LV00003B/945
* 9 7 9 8 2 3 3 6 3 4 2 5 3 *